Bill's for the Birds

Here's everything you need for something you'll never forget... the experience of a bird eating right out of your hand.

This book details how the idea for "Bill Bird-in-Hand" got its start...how Birds & Blooms Field Editors went about testing it... and how you, too, could be hand-feeding birds in no time at all.

BIRDS & BLOOMS BOOKS
Reiman Publications
Greendale WI 53129

"Is this close enough?"

CLOSE ENCOUNTER of the bird kind is enjoyed by Kelly Foley of Coopersburg, Pennsylvania, as a curious chickadee perches and peers into her lens. One of the joys of hand-feeding birds is how tame and comfortable they become around you. This especially delights children.

Bill's for the Birds

Editor: Roy Reiman

Assistant Editors: Jeff Nowak, Mandi Schuldt, Kristine Krueger

Art Director: Brian Sienko

Production Assistant: Ellen Lloyd

Birds & Blooms Books
© 2000 Reiman Publications, LLC
5400 S. 60th St., Greendale WI 53129

International Standard Book Number: 0-89821-297-9
All rights reserved.
Printed in U.S.A.

Notice: The information in this book has been gathered from a variety of people and sources, and all efforts have been made to ensure accuracy. Reiman Publications assumes no responsibility for any injuries suffered or damages or losses incurred as a result of this information. All information should be clearly understood before taking any action based on the information or advice in this book.

FOR ADDITIONAL COPIES of this book or information on other Reiman Publications books, see page 120. Or write: *Birds & Blooms* Books, P.O. Box 990, Greendale WI 53129-0990; call toll-free 1-800/558-1013 to order with a credit card; or visit our Web site at *www.reimanpub.com*.

What took 30 days may now take you only 30 minutes!

Field Editors who tested "Bill Bird-in-Hand" got those kind of results. But it's important to follow our directions closely based on their tests.

"I stood out in my yard last winter till my fingers turned blue, trying to convince chickadees that I am friendly enough for them to eat out of my hand. They didn't believe me! So I'm eager to see if Bill can do the trick."

—*Birds & Blooms* Field Editor Kathy Justy of Grafton, Ohio, prior to her test of "Bill".

MEET BILL. This is the very first prototype of "Bill Bird-in-Hand", set in the backyard of book's editor, Roy Reiman.

7

"It felt like a bit of heaven in my hand!"

"I watched and marveled as she sat on my hand. She would lose part of a seed between my fingers, then would nudge her beak between them until she found it again. It felt like a little bit of heaven in the palm of my hand!"

—Field Editor Barbara Dunn of Hollidaysburg, Pennsylvania, after quick success with the help of "Bill".

***You'll read dozens
of excited comments like this
throughout this book,
along with more tips and suggestions
on how you, too, can experience
"a little bit of heaven in your hand".***

Bill's Big Fun for a Bird Nut

By Roy Reiman

OKAY, I'll admit it. I'm a bird nut. As evidence, we have *27 birdhouses* in our front yard and at the edge of the woods behind our house.

I had no idea we had that many until one of our granddaughters, "Peanut", counted them during one of her visits. (Her real name's Kristin, but I've called her Peanut since the day she was born.)

After she finished tallying the birdhouses, she began counting the bird feeders, and I can't recall the number she came up with for those. But I'm sure there's close to a dozen.

In my defense—if one is needed—our home is very conducive to both birds and feeders. See, our home is set on the edge of 3 acres of thick woods just north of our company grounds. I walk through those woods on my way to work every day, down a winding path that forms sort of a leaf-covered "tunnel" between the house and our offices.

As a result, I'm fortunate to be able to enjoy a bit of nature on my way to and from work. I've had some enjoyable experiences during those treks and while working in my large garden on the other side of our driveway:

● "Bambi" and I have startled each other in the thick part of the woods several times. Bambi is the name we gave the fawn that was born just off our back deck a couple of years ago. She now comes back to our woods regularly to visit the salt block and nibble at the grain box I put out for her.

My wife, Bobbi, took several great photos of Bambi munching a few of my impatiens right outside our kitchen window. But I'll admit that as soon as she was done snapping those pictures, I shooed that "cute" deer away from my prized flowers!

● A pair of foxes had a den within 20 yards of my garden last year and they raised a litter of three. Sometimes when I came through the trees to the garden area, I'd find those little fellows lounging on the warm dirt next to my tomato plants.

And one morning we found one of them napping right on our front step. Bobbi got some good photos of that, too.

● A pair of great horned owls frequents our woods. Those birds are *huge* (up to 25 inches tall!). They sometimes wake us in the middle of the night with their back-and-forth *hoo, hoo-oo, hoo, hoo* calls. But we don't really mind.

> *"Someday before I die,"*
> *I thought to myself,*
> *"I'm going to—just once—*
> *get a bird to eat*
> *from my hand."*
> —Roy Reiman

We can only see them in silhouette in those wee hours, but it's easy to understand why they're often called the "cat owl". With their large head and upright ears, they look exactly like a huge cat from the neck up.

● We have a great variety of birds around our house, including Baltimore orioles (they went through eight oranges this spring), blue jays, black-capped chickadees, nuthatches,

American robins, downy woodpeckers, etc., plus lots of nesting house wrens. (How could anyone be in a bad mood when a wren is singing? Those busy little birds are my favorite.)

● We also have a lot more raccoons, woodchucks and opposums than we'd like. I probably wouldn't mind them so much if I wasn't a gardener.

How do these animals know *exactly* when a tomato or your sweet corn is ripe?? I wouldn't mind if they'd just take one of each and eat the whole thing, but no, they take just a bite or two of this one and that one and ruin the whole crop.

"Bill" Was Born in My Garden

Actually, it was out in that garden where this whole "Bill Bird-in-Hand" idea originated. I often refer to it as my "Therapy Garden", because it's where I get a lot of *thinking* done.

I know full well that I could buy these vegetables at the store for a lot less than I can grow them. (I had over $200 worth of new soil hauled into my garden this spring. How many years would it take before I could make that a good investment?)

But, just as with many other folks, that's not why I garden. I'm an ex-Iowa farm kid, and in a small way this is my "farm". I *love* going out there and digging in the soil…I like seeing radishes pop out of the ground in less than a week…I even

11

like seeing how straight the rows turn out, just as my dad took pride in having the straightest corn rows of any in our neighborhood.

> *"Right now, it could well be that fewer than one out of every million people has ever had a bird eat out of their hand. But in the months ahead, with 'Bill's' help, thousands of people may have that unforgettable experience."*

I can work up a real sweat in that garden… and in this modern age, when you live in a suburb with all of today's conveniences, there are few things that make you sweat anymore.

After an afternoon of gardening, I often ache in my shoulders and lower back, and I'm dead tired when I go to bed. But it's a *good* tired, one from physical exercise rather than mental strain, and I sleep better.

I guess that's the main reason I still hand-hoe the whole garden rather than use a mechanical tiller. It puts calluses on my hands and…well, I guess it helps the macho in me. (I used to wince when I shook hands with my Iowa farm brothers. They would notice and say, "Man, you have *soft* hands!" That doesn't happen when I'm gardening.)

There Must Be a Faster Way…

Anyway, it was while I was hoeing between the beets and the carrots one weekend that I came up with the idea for "Bill Bird-in-Hand".

I'd just finished editing some stories for *Birds & Blooms* the day before, in which people with more patience than I had described how—after a month or so of daily "training"—they had gotten birds to eat out of their hand.

Someday before I die, I thought to myself, *I'm going to—just once—get a bird to eat from my hand.*

The more I'd read of others achieving that, the more I

thought about what an unforgettable experience that must be. But then I asked myself, "When will I ever find time to devote an hour or so a day—for *20 or 30 days in a row*—to experience that on my own?" As busy as I seem to keep myself, the sobering answer was, "Probably never."

There must be a better, faster way to accomplish that, I thought. I started hoeing faster and thinking harder.

And that afternoon, out there in the garden, I came up with the concept for "Bill Bird-in-Hand". You're about to learn all about it in the pages ahead.

Consider this: If *you* find this exciting—as you read of the success the *Birds & Blooms* Field Editors had with the tests of our "Bill" prototypes—can you imagine how exciting all this is for *me*? It's the realization of a dream, the culmination of a "vision" I came up with out there in my garden.

Right now, it could well be that fewer than one out of every million people has ever had a bird eat out of their hand. But in the months ahead, as "Bill" gives people a hand, *thousands* of bird enthusiasts may have that unforgettable experience.

For me, that could be one of the most satisfying things I've ever achieved in an already highly satisfying career.

Does Hand-Feeding Endanger Birds?

Now and then a few people have raised some concern over the intrusive aspect of training birds to hand-feed. These folks fear that doing so might encourage birds to come within reach of people who could harm them.

This topic is addressed in detail in a later chapter in this book. But, because I don't want this concern to weigh on your mind as you read the pages just ahead, I want you to know that there is no evidence to suggest this is the case.

For example, bird authority Hugh Wiberg (you'll meet him in Chapter 10) has been hand-feeding birds—and teaching others how to do it—for more than 20 years. And he has yet to see or hear of a single instance in which a bird that has learned to hand-feed has been threatened or harmed by a human.

A lengthy study by the University of Wisconsin's Department of Wildlife Ecology validated that same conclusion.

What it comes down to is this: The kind of persons who care enough about birds to take the time to train them to hand-feed are not the type of people who would go out of their way to harm such a bird.

Nor do studies show that a bird becomes dependent on "handouts" once trained to feed from someone's hand. They go right back to looking for feed that's available elsewhere.

So don't let this concern about "intrusiveness" weigh on your mind as you read this book or put "Bill Bird-in-Hand" to work. Said one authority, "Hand-feeding wild birds is no more intrusive than setting up a bird feeder in your backyard."

Is "Bill" *Guaranteed* to Work?

No. This quick method is no more guaranteed to train birds to eat out of your hand than fishing lures guarantee you'll hook

A BLACK-CAPPED CHICKADEE perches on Bill's hand for a snack, obviously already comfortable with his presence.

a fish. There has to be fish in the area, and they have to be hungry.

The same is true for "Bill Bird-in-Hand". This quicker approach won't work unless there are birds in the area, and even then, it works best if there are the *right kind* of birds. Normally, chickadees, nuthatches and tufted titmice are the kind of bold little birds that can be most easily coaxed to your hand...by the "Bill method" or the traditional hand-feeding method.

> *"If everyone could get a bird to eat off their hand immediately, it wouldn't be such a novel, special experience. The 'not knowing', the trial and error, are all part of the fun..."*

If you don't have any of those three birds in your area, your chances of success may be reduced. Yet, as you'll see in the pages ahead, both my wife and I, as well as some of our testers, were able to draw in finches (normally a more skittish bird) on our *first* attempt after "training" with Bill.

On the other hand, whether you have success or not is part of the "fun" of attempting either training method. The "not knowing", the trial and error, the "I did it and you didn't" of this experience is also part of the enjoyment.

If *everyone* hit a home run the first time they came to bat, it wouldn't be special. Likewise, if *everyone* could get a bird to eat off their hand immediately, it wouldn't be such a novel, "special" experience. And it does take *patience*.

So, no, we can't *guarantee* you'll have success with "Bill Bird-in-Hand", but—as you'll learn in the pages ahead—*more than half* of our testers had *immediate* success with this approach.

While we can't guarantee "Bill" will work for you, I *can* guarantee that you, your whole family and even your neighbors will have a great deal of fun giving him a try.

In fact, Bill just may prove to be one of the best "conversation pieces" you ever put in your yard.

CONTENTS

CONTENTS

CONTENTS

CONTENTS

CONTENTS

CHAPTER 1

The Birth of "Bill"

AS I SAID in the Foreword (see page 9), this whole idea came to me one afternoon while I was hoeing weeds in my garden.

As regular readers of *Birds & Blooms* know, we've published a number of articles over the past couple of years about patient folks who have succeeded in getting birds to eat from their hands.

"Patience" is the operative word here, we've learned. In most cases, it takes several weeks or more before birds become bold enough to alight on someone's hand to snatch a snack.

Generally, the traditional technique goes like this: You observe when the birds' normal feeding period is…at mid-morning or whenever. Then, on your first day of "training" the birds, you stand *still as a statue* about 20 or 30 feet from your bird feeder for a half hour or more.

One Step at a Time

Each day thereafter, you move a step or so closer to your feeder until you're *finally* right next to it and the birds are still comfortable coming to it.

Then, when you feel the birds are "ready", you either empty or cover the feeder and put sunflower seeds (relished by chickadees and nuthatches, the two birds easiest to "train") on a plate, which you hold in your hand.

When a hungry bird spots the seed and is brave enough to eat from the plate, you're ready for the final stage: The next day, you put the seed directly in your hand and wait for your first "close encounter of the bird kind".

> *"The more I thought about it, the more I concluded the solution was to have someone or something do the waiting for me…"*

Problem is, while this method has proved effective and highly rewarding, not many people have the *time* for this traditional approach. It can take days and, in some cases, nearly a month…and even then it can take an hour or more *each day* you try this method.

Now, by contrast, wouldn't you be delighted if you could get birds to eat out of *your* hand…in the *first half hour*…on the *first day* you tried it?

That's What I Wondered…

As I was gardening that afternoon, I recalled how fascinated and excited *Birds & Blooms* readers have been about each of the "hand-feeding" articles we'd done. Unfortunately, though, I recognized that very few of them (and me!) would ever experience having a bird alight on their hand due to the time required to accomplish it.

Could I possibly come up with a way to reduce or totally eliminate that lengthy "training period" experts were saying it takes to get birds to eat from your hand?

The more I thought about it, the more I concluded that the solution would be to have someone or something *do the waiting for you.* As I mused and hoed and hoed and mused,

NOT PRETTY BUT EFFECTIVE. These are the original sketches Roy Reiman gave to several design firms when they first met to discuss his "Bill Bird-in-Hand" idea.

I suddenly recalled walking into a grocery store some time back and seeing an actual-size, cardboard version of "John Wayne" standing there.

"That's it! *That's it!*" I said out loud. Why not construct a human-size "dummy" to stand in your place for a week or two…then gradually move him closer to the feeder…and have him do the "training" for you?

It should work even *better* than the "regular" method, I thought, because the substitute is standing out there *all day*, not just an hour or so each day.

To start the process, you'd first put an old cap and shirt or coat on him—a cap and shirt you don't wear anymore—then set him about 20 or 30 feet away from your feeder. Each evening when you come home from work, you'd just move him a step or so closer, just as you'd do if you were standing there yourself using the traditional method.

Then, finally, when you have him right next to the feeder, and the birds are still comfortable coming to it, you'd close off the feeder and put seed in the dummy's hand. Once you see birds eating regularly from his hand, you're *ready*: You simply remove the dummy, slip on his shirt and hat and stand in his place. Now *that*, I felt, was an idea worth trying.

Called in Design Firms

With this concept in mind, we called in several large design firms. Most of these people were far from "bird nuts". I'll admit a few of them raised their eyebrows a bit at first when I showed them my sketches (at left) and described what I wanted—a "mannequin" that would stand out in the yard and attract birds to his hand!

But among this group was one fellow who was a bird enthusiast—he caught onto the concept immediately. I could see he was excited about it, not just from the business it might bring him, but from the sheer excitement of seeing whether this wild idea would work.

We established certain requirements for the prototype:

1. It had to be made of strong material and have a heavy coating to withstand the wind and other outdoor elements.

2. Since we wanted it to be about 5' 8" tall, it had to fold in the middle to make it easier to ship to direct-mail customers.

3. It had to have an "arm" that would be attached to the body by the customer.

4. This "arm" had to be sturdy, easy to assemble and attached in a way that allowed a shirt sleeve to fit over it.

5. The arm had to have a hand with a deep recessed area that would hold seed.

6. The mannequin had to have "loops" or brackets from head to toe along the back side for a pole (supplied with the unit) to be slid through. This pole would hold the body erect and be inserted into the ground to support the unit.

7. To keep the hat from blowing off, a special slot was needed at the back of the head for inserting the hatband.

8. We needed a face on the prototype, so we "drafted" one of the good-looking guys in our finance department, Paul Seubert, our company controller. (They have no sacred cows in that department, so his co-workers now delight in referring to him as "the dummy" whenever it's convenient.)

No Kitchen Sink?

House wrens select some mighty unusual materials to build their nests. One nest included 188 nails, 52 hairpins, 52 pieces of wire, 13 staples, 11 safety pins, six paper clips, four tacks, four pieces of pencil lead, three garter fasteners, two hooks and one buckle. (Sounds like these wrens were into heavy metal.)

With these instructions in hand, the design firm headed off to their plant. They said they'd be back in about a week with a preliminary model. We eagerly waited.

When they came back, we made some immediate small changes. But we liked what we saw the first day we met him. And we named him "Bill Bird-in-Hand".

We recorded the day, December 14, 1999. As far as we're concerned, Bill was born that day. And we'll celebrate his birthday on December 14. Anybody have a good recipe for a sunflower seed cake?

BIRDING BUDDIES. Roy Reiman, head of Reiman Publications, poses with an early prototype of "Bill Bird-in-Hand" shortly after it was put in place in his backyard.

THEY TAKING TURNS? Birds quickly become comfortable around "Bill Bird-in-Hand".

CHAPTER 2

Time to Put Bill to "The Test"

NOW that we had this single prototype of Bill Bird-in-Hand, we couldn't wait to test it. For credibility sake, we felt we shouldn't conduct the test ourselves. It needed to be some-one "off premise" and unbiased.

So, who should we pick to do it? It had to be someone we could trust...someone who would give it a *practical* test...someone who might even come up with suggestions to

HE'S CALLED "THE BIRDMAN". After considerable thought, we selected John Leeser from Macungie, Pennsylvania to conduct our first test of the "Bill" prototype.

improve the prototype.

In addition, we concluded, it would be ideal if we could choose someone who had trained birds to hand-feed the "traditional" way…and now see if Bill could reduce that time substantially.

With these goals in mind, we finally decided on John Leeser of Macungie, Pennsylvania. We'd featured John in our Premiere Issue of *Birds & Blooms* and had gotten so much response from readers that we did another photo-feature on him later, in December of 1999.

To many folks in his area, John is known as "The Birdman". For more than 20 years, he introduced fifth-grade students at a small school near Coopersburg to the joys of backyard bird feeding. He's now retired, but each winter John is invited back to teach a lesson about animal behavior.

Get-Acquainted Period

"When the weather turns colder in the fall, the students and I set up bird feeders in the wooded area next to Lower Milford Elementary School," he explains.

"Beginning in October, the pupils keep the feeders full of an assortment of seeds that birds relish. As the students fill the feeders each day, the birds become more and more trusting of them.

> *"We asked him to do it 'our way', by having Bill Bird-in-Hand do the extensive waiting and training for him…"*

"After several weeks of getting the birds comfortable with the presence of humans, the feeders are suddenly removed when the children are in the area. Then it's time to try to train the birds to eat out of

28

their hands. If a student stands very still, is patient and keeps a steady hand, a hungry bird might hop aboard for the first of what may be many visits.

"The students soon learn that the colder the temperature, the better the chances of a bird accepting their offering," he continues.

"I explain that since birds need more fuel to warm their bodies in cold weather, they're bolder when searching for food. This increases the chances of coaxing one to your hand.

"Hold Still, Stay Calm"

"Their first visitor will probably land close by and stare

at their offering. I tell them, '*Stay calm!* It's tough, but you can do it.' These young children need encouragement.

" 'Soon, your new friend may flutter above your hand a time or two to test your reaction,' I explain. 'When you gain its trust, get ready—the bird may quickly snatch a single seed from your open hand and head for the hills. Don't worry, it'll come back—and when it does, it'll likely stay longer each time.'

"I point out to them that hand-feeding gives you a rare chance to study a bird 'up close and personal'. You can see each species' colorful markings and plumage, physical structure and even notice its unique personality."

As the photos on these pages show, most of the students soon get many regular "close encounters" with birds of various kinds.

> ## Bird Bit
> Birds that nest in houses or cavities have a high rate of success. House wrens, for example, fledge about 79% of total eggs laid.

And once again, "The Birdman" has started yet another group of youngsters on their way to a life long interest in fully appreciating wild birds. Many of the students have told John years later that hand-feeding birds still remains one of their favorite school memories.

"Now Try It Our Way"

Now you can understand why we chose John for this first experiment with Bill Bird-in-Hand. He had more than 20 years of experience in feeding birds by hand and had taught hundreds of students to do the same.

But in each case, he'd done it the "regular" or "traditional" way, which in each case had usually had taken several weeks before the birds came to his or the students' hands.

John eagerly accepted the challenge. We asked him to do it "our way", eliminating the personal involvement by having Bill Bird-in-Hand do the extensive "waiting" and "training" for

FAVORITE PHOTO. The *Birds & Blooms* magazine staff has received *lots* of photos over the years, but they rank this one by John Leeser an all-time favorite. It's both humorous and poignant—just as this young girl was focusing her camera to get a shot of chickadees, one perched right on her lens to see what she was doing!

him, then making the switch when the birds were ready.

Because he felt the birds around the school might already be familiar with him, he decided to test it in his own back-yard, where he hadn't hand-fed birds before.

And, to further assure a "fair" test, he decided he'd have his daughter, Jaimie, stand in for Bill when he felt the birds were ready to try hand-feeding.

What's more, as you'll learn in the chapter just ahead, he eventually moved the prototype to another location at a near-by park for a second test.

WOULD BILL REALLY WORK? Readers have sent us photos like this one proving wild birds will eat from a human hand. But we needed John Leeser to send us photo proof that our "Bill method" really works. As you can see by the shot on the next page of his daughter, Jaimie, John conducted a picture-perfect test.

CHAPTER 3

Success First Time Out—It Worked!

NATURALLY, a lot of us here in our Wisconsin offices were anxiously waiting to hear how John Leeser's tests were going in Pennsylvania. After all, this little experiment had the potential of far-reaching results, as was immediately recognized by our *Birds & Blooms* Field Editors.

> *"Eventually the birds would spot me and actually fly to greet me and eat out of my hand!"*

We keep our Field Editors fully informed of our needs and activities (we have more than 100 of them across the U.S. and Canada), and they grasped the significance of this new approach to hand-feeding as soon as they heard about it.

"What a great human interest story!" wrote Phil Ahrens of

Huntingburg, Indiana in a typical comment. "This project has the potential of giving thousands of people the personal experience of getting a bird to eat from their hand."

Other Field Editors wanted to hear how the test fared for personal reasons. "I stood out in my yard last winter till my fingers turned blue, trying to convince chickadees that I'm friendly enough for them to eat out of my hand," related Kathy Justy of Grafton, Ohio. "They didn't believe me! So I'm eager to see if Bill Bird-in-Hand can do the trick."

None were as eager as we were!

We were pretty excited when the call finally came in from

BILL GIVES BIRD A HAND. It wasn't long after John Leeser put Bill in his Pennsylvania backyard that birds like this little chickadee began eating seed from his hand.

John. "It worked," he said, sounding a lot more calm than we were. "In fact, it worked on the *first try*, and I have plenty of photo evidence. I shot more than 20 slides of my daughter hand-feeding chickadees."

"Well, how long did it take?" we asked. "How did you go about it? Did you do it like we recommended?" Our questions bubbled out.

The answers were just what we wanted to hear. We learned that our prototype had reduced the usual 2-or-more week training period normally needed

"HELLO THERE!" On her *first try*, Jaimie Leeser had a chickadee eat from her hand. (Note she wore the same shirt and hat Bill was wearing.)

to convert birds to hand-feeding to *less than an hour* on the *first day*!

John said he began by putting Bill Bird-in-Hand some distance from the feeder in his backyard. Emulating the traditional method, he moved Bill a little closer to the feeder each day for the next week or more.

He noticed and pointed out to us an advantage over the "human method" that we hadn't considered: The birds seemed to become comfortable with Bill's presence more quickly, because Bill was out there *throughout the day*, rather than just for a half hour or so, as is usually the case with any busy person. Finally, when he got Bill positioned right next to the feeder and the birds kept coming in for snacks, he moved to stage two. He emptied the feeder and put seed in the special cavity built into Bill's hand. Then he watched.

"Where'd It Go??"

When the birds—mostly chickadees—returned and found the feeder empty, it wasn't long before they spotted the seed in Bill's hand. They soon perched on Bill's cap, his shoulders, then hopped to his hand. John knew the birds were now ready for "The Test".

The next morning, he went out just before the birds arrived and removed Bill from the site. Then his daughter, Jaimie, volunteered to put on Bill's shirt and cap and stand in his place.

Bird Bit
The heart of a hummingbird beats 20 times faster than a human heart.

"Soon several curious chickadees landed on the empty feeder," John said. "It didn't take long before the friendly little fellows *hopped onto her hand*! It was neat to see the surprised expression on her face.

"I think you can tell from the pictures she was pretty pleased. (See pages 33 and 35.) And the birds kept coming back to her hand for more, even though I was close enough to shoot a lot of pictures to record the moment."

While Jaimie was "pretty pleased", we were *incredibly* pleased to learn that Bill Bird-in-Hand, on his very first test, had reduced the usual training time requirement from *weeks* to *minutes*.

That is, instead of having to personally stand out in cold weather for an hour or so daily for 2 to 3 weeks…we knew any bird lover could now have Bill do the waiting, then accomplish the same thing by switching places with him…and get a bird on his or her hand in a matter of minutes!

John and Jaimie soon discovered other benefits—they learned that once the birds were at ease with them, they no longer had to assume Bill's pose in order to feed them.

"The birds eventually started following us around the backyard, looking for a handout!" John reported. "In fact, I moved Bill to a nearby park for a second test, just to be sure this first one wasn't a fluke. I got the same results.

"Eventually I began putting seed in my pocket each time

BROTHER GIVES IT A TRY. After Jaimie's success, Barrie Leeser, John's brother, took a turn at convincing a chickadee to eat from his hand. The photo says it all!

I stepped out of my car at the park. On some occasions, the chickadees would spot me and actually fly out to the parking lot to greet me! Each time, I gladly rewarded them with a hand-fed treat."

While this success had only happened at one test area, we knew we had a unique concept with Bill Bird-in-Hand that was worth pursuing. So we immediately filed for a patent for both the product and the method.

That patent is now pending. We also filed for a trademark of the "Bill Bird-in-Hand" name.

The excitement among our staff was escalating.

FUN FOR THE WHOLE FAMILY. Once Bill got the birds trained, everyone in the Leeser family got involved in having birds eat from their hand. Here Jane Leeser, John's wife, experiences the special feeling of a chickadee perched on her hand.

CHAPTER 4

More Tests Needed...to Make Sure

OKAY, our first Bill Bird-in-Hand prototype had worked even better than we'd dreamed. But that was a *single* test.

We felt we needed to check it out more thoroughly before we considered offering this product to subscribers to *Birds & Blooms* magazine, as well as to the more than 2 million people who receive our Country Store direct-mail catalog in spring and fall each year.

So, we decided to have a group of our Field Editors across the country put a unit to the test. We would have loved to have had every one of those 100-plus bird enthusiasts check it out, but it was too costly.

That first prototype had cost us nearly $3,000 to design and produce. Now, going back to the same design firm, we learned that any fewer than 200 units would cost us $300 apiece, due to all the handwork on such a short-run basis.

> *"We recognized time was precious—it was already March, and the colder the temperature, the better our chances..."*

After talking to members of our finance department (they always tend to pull back our reins but never dim our enthusiasm for "wild" ideas like this), we decided we'd turn out 20 of them, investing another $6,000 in the project.

Now, which 20 Field Editors should we ask to test these units? We assumed that every one of these "bird nuts" would want to get involved if we asked, so rather than stir up all of them, we decided to elect and contact 60 of them—geographically sprinkled throughout the country—to see if Bill worked as well in different regions. In late February, we sent each of them a lengthy letter describing the project. We told them we had only 20 units and wanted to know who among them would be interested in working with us on this test.

Here's What We Told Them

The following is the exact text of that letter we sent to the 60 Field Editors we selected:

February 25, 2000

Good Morning!

We need the help of a few of our Field Editors for a unique bird-feeding test. Please read the following details, and then let us know if you'd like to be considered for part of our "test group".

We've developed a revolutionary new way to teach birds to eat out of your hand, and now we need a group of enthusiastic Field Editors to help us put it to the test in "real" backyards across the country.

Here's some background:

A few months ago, one of our editors came up with a really unique idea. After seeing photos and articles about B&B readers feeding chickadees and other backyard birds from their hands, he wanted to enjoy this magical experience himself.

However, he'd learned from these articles that it could take several weeks before a bold bird might eat seed from his hand. In addition to the kind of patience that would require, his job

wouldn't permit him to be in his backyard during the weekday hours needed to "train" these birds.

That dilemma sparked an idea that, if successful, would allow him to get birds to eat out of his hand in ONE DAY. Since he couldn't be in the backyard while most birds are feeding, he decided to produce a full-size "dummy" to stand in his place for a week or more and do the waiting for him!

Then, when the birds are comfortable feeding from the mannequin's hand, all our editor would have to do on a weekend is slip on the dummy's clothes and take its place.

With this concept in mind, we've developed "Bill Bird-in-Hand", a self-standing, weatherproof human-size dummy that takes only 5 minutes to set up. Again, our hope is that after a week or so, birds will become comfortable eating out of Bill's hand...and then any avid bird feeder can don Bill's shirt and hat at their convenience and have birds eating out of their own hand.

Will it work? Well, it already did in our first test.

We sent the prototype of Bill to one of our B&B Field Editors, John Leeser of Macungie, Pennsylvania. He gave it a thorough test, and it worked like a charm (see photo evidence enclosed).

He sent us pictures of birds first feeding from Bill's hand...and then feeding from his daughter's hand when she donned Bill's same shirt and hat and stood in his place.

NOW WE'RE EXPANDING THIS TEST so we can find out if it works in backyards throughout the country. And we'd like to know if YOU would be interested in helping us with this project.

The test shouldn't be difficult—we'll send you Bill (he stands about 5' 8") and complete instructions explaining how to set him up in your backyard. In minutes, he'll be waiting for birds.

Then we'll ask you to keep an eye on Bill and take notes: How long did it take before birds perched on Bill's hand? What time of day did they feed the most from his hand? How long did you wait before you (or another family member) donned Bill's cap and shirt and took his place? How long did it take before birds were as comfortable coming to your hand as they'd become to Bill's?

We'll also ask you to take some photos of Bill and then the "stand-in" person (wearing Bill's clothes) with a bird eating from his/her hand to prove the process worked for you.

Down the line, our ultimate goal is to offer this unique "Bill Bird-in-Hand" to all bird enthusiasts so that they, too, can enjoy the experience of having a bird eat out of their hand within <u>hours</u> rather than <u>weeks</u>.

If and when we do, we'll share your best tips and hints that will make this feeder work even better for them. Just think of the fun and enjoyment hundreds of people will have feeding birds from their hands right in their backyards!

But, before we get ahead of ourselves, we want to have this approach tested in various parts of the country so we have more experience to draw on if and when we market this unit.

If <u>you</u> would like to be one of the Field Editors considered for

this trial, please return the enclosed form and describe your in-terest as soon as possible. If you're not interested in trying it, fine, because we don't have enough prototypes (we only have 20) for all our Field Editors. We'll select several in each region of the country from those who say "yes", indicating they're will-ing to try "Bill Bird-in-Hand" in their backyard.

Thanks for reading this long letter. We think this will be an ex-citing "field test", and if those who participate have the kind of success that our Pennsylvania tester, John Leeser, did, hun-dreds and maybe thousands of people across the country will have the unforgettable experience of feeding a wild bird from their hand for the first time.

Sincerely,

Jeff Nowak, Editor
Birds & Blooms

Time Was of the Essence

When we'd assumed in advance that most of our Field Ed-itors would immediately say "yes" to our offer, we'd guessed right. No fewer than *40* of the 60 quickly responded saying they'd *love* to give Bill Bird-in-Hand a try!

We carefully screened these re-sponses for enthusiasm and location, selected 20 and then began putting pressure on the design firm to hurry in turning out those 20 prototypes.

We recognized that time was pre-cious—it was already March.

John Leeser's words echoed in our

ears: "The colder the temperature, the better the chances of a bird accepting your offering. Birds need more fuel to warm their bodies in cold weather, and they're bolder when searching for food. This increases your chances of coaxing one to your hand during lower temperatures."

Likewise, cold weather increased our chances of success with Bill. We knew that the warmer the weather got in each of these test areas, the less we could count on birds visiting ancillary feed sources. C'mon...*hurry!*

***BRRR!* BUT BETTER BILL THAN YOU!** Bill Bird-in-Hand is one tough hombre when it comes to cold and snow. He'll stand out there doing his job while everyone else is huddled around the fireplace. Actually, as emphasized by John Leeser, birds are more likely to hand-feed during colder months when feed is harder for them to find.

CHAPTER 5

Lots of Excitement in the Mail

WE WERE AMAZED at the excited response from Field Editors to our "Bill Bird-in-Hand Letter", as we referred to it here in our offices.

Not only did *more than 40* of the 60 respond within a week with an enthusiastic "Yes!", almost all of them sent along personal comments on how much *fun* this test would be.

Here are just a few sample comments from those who looked forward to giving Bill Bird-in-Hand a try in their backyard:

> *"I'm dying to try it. I haven't had the time to try to teach birds to eat from my hand the regular way..."*

"Ever since I read the story in the Premiere Issue of *Birds & Blooms* about the teacher showing his students how to get birds to eat from their hands, I've been dying to try it," wrote Barbara Dunn of Hollidaysburg, Pennsylvania.

"But I haven't had that kind of time," she said. "Bill Bird-in-Hand is the best bird-feeding idea I've heard of yet!"

Sounds Good to Her

"I've tried to get birds to eat out of my hand, but I lost patience. Plus, my arm got tired from waiting so long," Debora Saulsgiver of Procious, West Virginia penned. "I'm interested in seeing if your unique 'shortcut' really works."

And the excitement went on as we continued reading Field Editor responses, some almost *begging* us to choose them for this trial. Honestly, we got a little concerned that some of them would be offended if they weren't among those selected.

So...we wrote to *all* 100-plus of our *B&B* Field Editors and

EVERYONE WANTED TO GET INVOLVED. The arrival of the "Bill" prototype at the 20 selected testers' homes caused a lot of excitement in their neighborhoods. Above, a neighbor friend of Iowa Field Editor Wendell Obermeier came over to help set it up.

shared complete details about the "Bill test". We decided to do so because we were planning to print an article on the project in an upcoming issue of *Birds & Blooms*, and since readers often ask our Field Editors questions, we wanted all of them to be fully informed.

We then explained that we'd carefully selected 20 of the Field Editors who volunteered, primarily based on their geographical distribution. And we quickly added this:

"We're sorry to disappoint the rest of you who said yes, but we make this promise to you and ALL other Field Editors:

"If and when we go into mass production of Bill Bird-in-Hand, each of you Field Editors will be the first to receive a FREE unit to put to good use in your backyard. Fair enough?"

That worked. All of them were more than satisfied with that offer. (Multiple units of Bill are being manufactured as this is being written, and the first ones completed will be sent to those Field Editors who weren't involved in the test.)

Wanted Opinion of an "Expert"

In the process of testing Bill, we made contact with Hugh Wiberg of Wilmington, Massachusetts. Hugh had recently published a book, *Hand-Feeding Backyard Birds*, and he'd sent us a copy to review.

I personally read it cover to cover on the very evening it arrived. I thoroughly enjoyed it—to my knowledge, it's the only book on hand-feeding published to date.

Hugh's book includes a step-by-step guide on how to train birds to hand-feed the traditional way. It's effective, but it involves a considerable amount of time.

For example, I learned from his book that Hugh began his training process on Saturday and Sunday mornings in November in the back-yard of his home. For the first three weekends, he stood near a maple tree about 15 feet from his feeder, spending 20 to 30 minutes each time.

> **Bird Bit**
> During nesting season,
> male pileated woodpeckers
> may spend 18 hours
> a day incubating eggs.

On the fourth Saturday, he moved five paces toward the feeder and "turned into a statue". On each succeeding Saturday, he closed the gap by a foot or two.

By the sixth Saturday, Hugh was standing only 4 feet away. With little hesitation, chickadees soon busied them-

selves at the feeder. And on the eighth weekend, they finally ate from his hand.

Would He Try It "Our Way"?

After finishing the book, I gave Hugh a call and we had a very pleasant visit. (Two "bird nuts" talking on the phone can go on about as long as two grandmothers talking

about grandkids.)

I described my "shortcut" approach of Bill Bird-in-Hand to Hugh, and he eagerly asked if he could have one of the prototypes to test.

Since we put a high value on his opinion, we scrambled around to get still one more Bill turned out by the manufacturer.

We shipped it to

IN HANDS OF AN EXPERT. Bird authority Hugh Wiberg (above) was very eager to give Bill a try.

Hugh, and he made a point to test it in an area where birds were unfamiliar with him. Hugh kept a "diary" of his test with Bill, which you'll read in Chapter 10.

> *"They all commented on how much __fun__ this test would be..."*

But we will give you this sneak preview: On the day that he removed Bill and stood in his place, Hugh had a chickadee eating out of his hand *in just 10 minutes!*

FAMILY PHOTO? The Field Editors selected to test Bill were elated. When they set up the prototype, many—like Wendell "Obie" Obermeier here—even posed with him. (In a later chapter, you'll learn something happened to this particular Bill.)

NEIGHBORHOOD PRANK? While members of the test group enjoyed the notoriety of being selected to try out Bill Bird-in-Hand, they sometimes had to put up with some ribbing by friends, like this flock of phony birds someone placed on Bill's hand.

CHAPTER 6

If All Else Fails, Read the Directions

UNFORTUNATELY, this old expression (above) sometimes has more truth than humor to it.

We didn't want that to be the case with the Bill Bird-in-Hand prototypes we were shipping to our Field Editors. We had far too much at stake. So we put our instructions on the *outside* of the package and urged the editors to read them thoroughly even before they unpacked Bill.

Later, we learned those who did exactly that—and then carefully followed our detailed directions—were among those who had success with the unit. Those who "sorta" followed our directions were only "sorta successful".

> *"After the birds become accustomed to taking food from your hand, I recommend that you talk softly to them and gradually get them used to some small, slow movements…"*

(That being the case, we *strongly advise* anyone who orders and uses one of our Bill Bird-in-Hand units should follow our detailed instructions carefully.)

The directions we're talking about are these, verbatim as we sent them to those 20 Field Editors:

Important to Do It *Right*

After you get Bill Bird-in-Hand unpackaged and assembled (which shouldn't take long with our easy-to-follow instructions), here is the best way to proceed, based on what we've learned to date.

You already know the customary approach to hand-feeding…"training" the birds over several weeks by gradually standing closer and closer to your feeder for an hour or so each

ALMOST READY. Whole families got involved in the testing of Bill. Here, Rosalie Johnson, sister of tester Liz McCain of Florence, Oregon, puts seed in Bill's hand.

day…then finally getting the birds to eat from your hand when they're comfortable with your presence right next to the feeder.

Again, this traditional method takes a lot of time and patience. By contrast, the ultimate goal of Bill Bird-in-Hand is to reduce that waiting period to a <u>single</u> <u>day</u>, maybe even to a <u>single</u> <u>hour</u>, and have success the <u>first</u> <u>time</u> you change places with Bill.

We've already told you that's exactly how it worked for John Leeser, the first one to test this approach. Let's hope it works just as well for you.

Here are some things we learned from John's test in Pennsylvania and through our own tests. We urge you to follow these suggestions closely:

1. Bill Bird-in-Hand works best when he's placed in the proximity of your most popular feeder, where birds are already accustomed to coming. Chickadees, nuthatches and tufted titmice are the easiest to train for hand-feeding, so choose the feeder that already attracts these birds.

2. We learned it helps immensely if you choose a feeder near a "surveillance tree" or trees—preferably <u>behind</u> Bill so birds later approach you from the <u>back</u>. This allows birds to first light and observe the situation before going to the feeder.

3. The more you can emulate the "normal" training techniques of the traditional hand-feeding approach, the better your chances of success. Therefore, it's best to first put Bill 20 or so feet away from the feeder, then every few days move him closer, just as is recommended when a human "trains" the birds.

Moving him now and then may take some effort, but keep in mind it sure beats the <u>hours</u> you would spend standing out there in person. If moving him is difficult for you—due to driving Bill's support stake into frozen ground, e.g.—perhaps you could at least try three moves —one 20 feet or so away, then at a midpoint, then next to feeder.

4. *Since Bill's doing the waiting instead of you, you may be in less of a hurry to gradually move him closer; you may even want to begin with him farther away.*

When we tested one of the units here near our offices, we started with Bill right next to the feeder, just to see what would happen. That totally scared the birds away, and they avoided the feeder completely. But even in that we saw something positive: We knew then the birds apparently regarded Bill as "human".

5. *We recommend that you **don't put seed in Bill's hand until you finally have him next to the feeder**. Even then, it's better to wait to put seed in his hand until just a day or two before you plan to change places with him.*

(This is particularly important if you have squirrels in your area; if squirrels climb on Bill to "check him out" and find feed there, they'll keep coming back and eventually damage Bill's arm. If they check earlier and nothing's there, they'll like-

ly leave him alone and won't be a bother when you're finally ready to "plant" seed in Bill's hand.)

6. *John Leeser, our Pennsylvania tester, came up with a good idea we hadn't thought of. He added extra support to Bill's arm by standing a metal plant hanger (shepherd's hook) in front of the unit so Bill's hand could rest on it (see photo at left).*

Not only did this keep squirrels, etc. from weakening Bill's arm as they investigated it, but

STEADY HAND. We noticed in this photo from John Leeser that he'd put a shepherd's hook under Bill's hand to steady it. Hmmm...not a bad idea.

"This prop steadies your hand later when you switch places with Bill," John pointed out. (Ed-

itor's Note: If you use Bill in a _sitting_ position—see Chapters 11 and 12—choose a chair with _armrests_ for the same reason.)

7. When, after a week or more, you've succeeded in moving Bill right next to your feeder (in one of our own tests, at that point we wired Bill's shoulder to the side of the feeder for extra support), you're finally ready for "THE TEST": Seeing if birds will eat from your hand!

8. The words of John Leeser at this stage of his test were so exciting we'll just quote him here: "On the day you try hand-feeding, you should go outdoors before the birds usually arrive. It's important to empty the feeder or cover the feed in the feeder. This will focus the bird's attention on the feed in your hand.

> **"When the birds get comfortable with you, you no longer have to assume Bill's pose. We found the birds eventually started following us around the backyard looking for a handout!"**

"Remove Bill Bird-in-Hand and get him totally out of sight, then wear his cap and shirt. When you take his place, you must stand as motionless as possible, in the same pose and position as Bill. Fill your hand with fresh sunflower kernels…and wait.

"In my case, when my daughter stood in for Bill, several chickadees first landed on the feeder or the plant hanger in front of her. But it didn't take long before the friendly little fellows hopped onto her hand for her first experience at hand-feeding!"

9. John added these interesting comments: "Once you get them eating from your hand, the more time you spend with them, the more they will trust you.

"After the birds become accustomed to taking food from your hand, I recommend that you talk softly to them and gradually make some small, slow movements.

"When the birds get comfortable with that, you no longer

have to assume Bill Bird-in-Hand's pose. We found the birds eventually started following us around the backyard looking for a handout!"

The Same Could Happen to You

See how exciting this procedure can be...and what it can lead to? The instructions we just shared—the very ones we sent to the 20 Field Editors on our test team—proved very helpful.

These testers reported that these recommended steps had a great deal of merit; the closer these instructions were followed, the better the test worked.

The same will surely prove true for all others who put Bill Bird-in-Hand to work in their backyards.

Great Reaction from Readers

AS SOON as the article about the tests of Bill Bird-in-Hand appeared in Birds & Blooms magazine, we began receiving mail from subscribers about this interesting experiment. Here's a typical letter:

"I cannot tell you how thrilled and excited I am to read about Bill Bird-in-Hand. All I can say is that I absolutely have to have one as soon as they're ready.

"With my long workweeks, I simply haven't found suffi-cient time to get the birds to cooperate in the normal time-tested way. This looks like it could be the answer for me and other busy people.

"Thank you for this great idea! When I read about this, it made my whole week, not just my day."

—Ellen Lawson, Lawrenceville, Georgia

CHAPTER 7

Testers Come Up with Ideas of Their Own

EACH of the 20 members of the test team was sent complete step-by-step assembly instructions. Yet, we made a point that if, after putting Bill together, they came up with any suggestions to make the task even easier, they should let us know.

They did. Some of their suggestions were excellent, and we've now

> ## Bird Bit
> Nearly half of the birds in the world migrate, spending the year in two different locations.

incorporated them as part of the clear, concise directions that accompany each Bill Bird-in-Hand package.

Below and on the next pages are just a few of the photos and instructions incorporating the suggestions—such as a

Photo 1

new sturdier and easier-to-attach wooden arm—from members of our test team.

Several of these testers told us later they really appreciated and *used* our three "Staking It Out" ideas to make the support for Bill sturdier and easier to move. (Those three ideas are on page 61.)

Ready...Set...Assemble

It shouldn't take you more than 10 or 15 minutes to have Bill Bird-in-Hand ready to go to "work" for you if you follow these step-by-step directions.

Here's all you need to get started: A hammer, a Phillips screwdriver, one loose-fitting shirt or jacket and one cap or hat.

(We suggest you choose an old cap and a shirt or coat you don't use anymore—one that will comfortably fit *over* other clothing when you're ready to switch places and stand in for Bill.)

Photo 2

Photo 1 shows how Bill Bird-in-Hand should look when you're finished assembling him. Here are the easy steps to get him to this stage:

1. Unfold Bill to full height and lay facedown on the grass or carpet. (Before assembling, you may want to improve Bill's appearance as you can see we did in photo 1 on page 57—we used a permanent marker to draw pant creases, cuffs and shoes onto Bill.)

2. Bend the horizontal tabs at the waist and feet away from the body. (Shown at bottom of photo 2.)

3. Bend and fold the shoulder support to form a rectangular box (photo 2). When properly folded, the hole for the support pipe will be at the *bottom* of the box.

Remove the protective facing from the glue tab and press

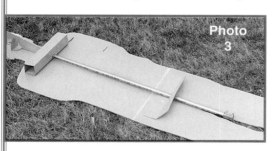

Photo 3

it into place. This will keep the shoulder support from unfolding.

4. Place the pipe connector (shown at the far right in photo 3) on the end of one of the sections of pipe and tighten it with a screwdriver. Insert the other end of that same pipe (the end without the connector) through the waist tab and up into the shoulder support.

The top of the pipe should be against the top of the rectangular box, and the pipe connector should be located below the waist tab (as shown in photo 3). The bottom section of pipe will be added later.

5. You're now ready to locate Bill Bird-in-Hand in your backyard about 20 or 30 away from a feeder that birds frequent. (If you have a choice, choose a feeder that's close to trees or shrubs, which will provide birds protective cover as they investigate Bill. We've learned this is a big aid to success.)

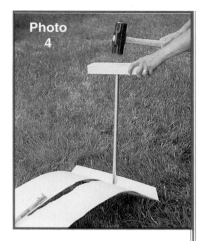

Photo 4

6. Lay Bill facedown (photo 4), placing his feet exactly where you want him to stand. Insert the bottom section of pipe through the hole in the horizontal tab near Bill's feet and pound the pipe into the ground about 10 inches deep.

(Be sure to place a scrap block of wood over the top of the pipe so you don't damage it while pounding. In fact, if your ground is unusually hard, you may want to first read the additional "Staking It Out" tips that follow.)

7. Holding the top pipe, lift Bill to an upright, standing position. Slide the pipe connector of his back support onto the lower pipe and tighten with a screwdriver.

8. Using the two enclosed glue tabs, remove the protective facing from one side of each one and press them onto the back of Bill's wooden arm (shown in photo 5 on page 60). One should be placed near the top of the arm and the other near the elbow. Once in place, remove the second side of the protective tabs and press the arm into place on Bill, just below shoulder. The arm can be

> *"Consider doing what some of us Wisconsinites do during winter months —use an electric drill to start the holes in the soil."*

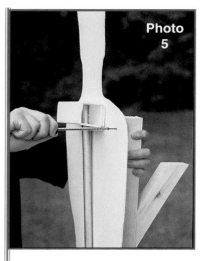

Photo 5

placed on Bill's left side if you're left-handed.

For additional strength, you may want drive two screws into Bill's wooden arm from behind (photo 5).

9. Place the decal of Bill's face onto his body. Be sure that the surface area is clean and dry before putting it on. (To easily separate the protective backing from the decal, crease a small corner on Bill's neck.)

10. Dress Bill in the same loose-fitting shirt or light jacket that you plan to wear later when you stand in for him.

Insert Bill's arm through the sleeve of the shirt. (Note: Before buttoning shirt, you may want to "bulk up" Bill's body by stuffing paper or towels inside plastic bags to stay dry.)

11. Attach Bill's hand to his arm by screwing it in place from the top of his hand (photo 6).

12. Place a hat or cap on Bill's head. To keep it from blowing off, tape or staple it to the back of Bill's head. If you live in a windy area, you may want to use tape or some other means to hold down the *front* of Bill's cap as well. (We're talking from experience here in windy Wisconsin.)

Photo 6

You're now ready to put Bill Bird-in-Hand to task. It might be good to reread "Important to Do It Right" (page 51) before you put Bill to work.

STAKING IT OUT
(Well Worth Reading)

AS WE ADVISED in our list of "Important to Do It Right" suggestions (page 51), it's best to start with "Bill" some distance from your feeder and then gradually move him closer.

If repositioning him periodically is difficult because you have hard, rocky or frozen soil in your area, here are several ways to make it easier to drive in Bill's support stake initially, and to move him to different spots later:

1. The pipe supporting Bill is lightweight conduit, about 1/2" in diameter, and therefore, it won't withstand heavy pounding. So you may want to use a scrap piece of heavier pipe to make the hole in the ground (10" down is adequate), then remove it and insert Bill's lighter conduit stake into the hole. Then fill in soil around pole and tamp it solid.

2. Or, consider doing what some of us Wisconsinites do during winter months: Use an electric or hand drill with a twist bit (the kind used to drill in wood) to drill a 1/2" or larger hole in

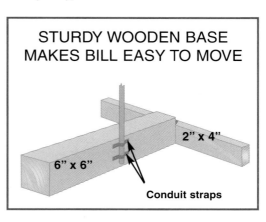

STURDY WOODEN BASE MAKES BILL EASY TO MOVE

2" x 4"

6" x 6"

Conduit straps

the soil. Works like a charm—you'll be done in a jiffy.

In fact, you may want to drill all of the holes for Bill's different positions the first time out—that way you'll have them all ready ahead of time.

3. Or, consider eliminating the need for ground holes completely by constructing a wooden stand made from a 3- to 4-foot 6" x 6" with a 3- to 4-foot 2" x 4" crosspiece (as shown in sketch above). Use two conduit straps to attach Bill's support pipe to the wooden stand. (Cut off about 10 inches of the lower pipe using a hacksaw.)

This portable base makes it easy to move Bill frequently, gradually edging him nearer the feeder and improving your chances!

WHAT A THRILL! For people who are really "into birds", few things match the excitement of having a wild bird eat from their hand. Note how the cute little nuthatch in this picture has one of its toes wrapped around this feeder's finger. What a feeling!

> *"The first time it happens, it's really something!"*
> —Barbara Dunn

CHAPTER 8

Here's the Best Part of This Book!

YOU'LL LIKELY ENJOY this chapter more than any other
…just as we enjoyed hearing the exciting success stories from
our test team members more than anything that had happened up to this point.

Some of them were so exhilarated the first time they succeeded at getting a bird on their hand they couldn't wait to
write. They *called* us! Others E-mailed. Not just once, but several times as they had new experiences and success with Bill.

Typical was the comment of Barbara Dunn from Hollidaysburg, Pennsylvania (shown below): "I watched and mar-

63

veled. It felt like a little bit of heaven in the palm of my hand.

"Within just a *half hour* after I traded places with Bill, I had a female American goldfinch on my hand!"

Even we were amazed at Barbara's success with a *goldfinch*, because it was the first time we'd heard of anyone succeeding with anything other than chickadees, nuthatches and tufted titmice, which are by nature some of the friendliest birds. Goldfinch are normally "skittish", the females more so than the males. Yet, that's the first bird that came to Barbara's hand.

"She ate and ate," Barbara related. "She was so comfortable that I could feel the warmth of her belly on my hand. It was *awesome*. She would lose part of a seed between my fingers and nudge her beak between them until she found it again."

Then Barbara added the comment we heard again and again from test team members: "Thank you for a first-time experience I will never forget!"

Whole Neighborhoods Got Involved

We could tell from their responses that these tests had effects far beyond just training birds to eat from their hands.

These Field Editors were enjoying a great sense of *involvement*...they felt like "pioneers", trying a new idea that might be emulated by thousands...they felt a responsibility to play by the rules and give us honest, usable feedback.

And in some cases, they became minor "celebrities" in their neighborhood when people spotted Bill Bird-in-Hand in their yard and got curious.

"We had a house full of company over the weekend and Bill became the center of attention," reported one tester. "He's just about the best conversation piece I've ever seen!"

"Our bird feeders are in our front yard, so we put Bill out there for our tests," related another. "We had no idea the fuss it would cause. Cars slowed down…some stopped…and a few got so curious they pulled in our driveway and apologetically said they couldn't resist asking what that 'guy' was doing out there.

"We've made some new friends among birders through Bill. He's sort of becoming a member of our family!"

Written Up in Local Papers

Some members of our test team were even featured in their local newspaper (sample below). Word of this "bird experiment" started spreading through town and eventually reached the desk of a local reporter who thought it sounded interesting.

Probably the most unusual situation involved one of our Iowa testers, who got extended press coverage he never expected: His "Bill" was *abducted* from his yard one night! We're guessing the local police decided to have a little fun with it, because they put out an APB (All Points Bulletin) regarding the "Bill-napping". Whatever the

Birds do flock together at local couple's home

By Benjamin Kostka
Press Staff Writer

Long-time Charles City residents Wendell and Marilyn Obermeier probably have more friends than any one person could ever ask for. For almost 19 years the couple has enjoyed the company of friends who appear in all colors, shapes and sizes.

These 'friends' aren't people though, rather they might be called the Obermeier's fine feathered friends.

Yes, the Obermeier's backyard plays host on a daily basis as the area's many birds whistle their way through their own personal haven.

"I got started with watching birds way back when I was in Boy Scouts," mentioned Wendell Obermeier. "Marilyn has been doing this since she was in grade school. It's great that we both share this common interest."

Being that Wendell is a Field Editor for *Birds and Blooms* magazine, the Obermeier's have recently acquired a new addition to their circle of friends, though this one is not feathered form.

"I was chosen to receive a 'Bill Bird-in-Hand' feeder along with

only 20 other field editors throughout different regions of the United States," mentioned Obermeier. "The goal of the feeder is to get birds to feed right out of your hand."

This prototype is the first known of its kind to ever be produced and according to Obermeier, it could possibly be marketed throughout the country pending its success.

"I will be getting in touch with the magazine after a while to let them know how things are going with 'Bill'," remarked Obermeier. "If this really turns out to work, who knows, everyone may have a chance to own one of these."

"So far we haven't had much of a response, but I don't really think the birds have gotten used to the idea of it yet," he continued. "Hopefully, though, once they do, maybe they might eat out of our hands too."

The figure is also clothed in an outfit similar to one which either Wendell or Marilyn might wear when feeding the birds. In 'Bill's' hand' there is a small area designed to hold food.

Birdfeeder

Continued on page 2

Birds get a 'handout'

Wendell and Marilyn Obermeier of Charles City have enjoyed bird watching for decades and have just recently acquired what they hope will attract even more birds to their backyard. 'Bill Bird-in-Hand', a life-size human cutout, will be put to the test by the Obermeiers and Wendell will report the results back to *Birds and Blooms*, a magazine for which he is a field editor. The figure is designed to allow birds to become used to eating right out of a person's hand.

Press photo by Benjamin Kostka

TICKLING HIS SHOULDER. A nuthatch eyes seed in Bill's hand. Note how this test team member added a shepherd's plant hook *behind* Bill to help stabilize him.

case, Bill is still missing as this is being written. You will learn more of the lighthearted details on this in Chapter 13.

Some testers were even asked to speak at schools and area meetings when their project became known.

"I did a presentation for a group of seniors at my church on this project and my experiences as a Field Editor," wrote Sue Gronholz of Beaver Dam, Wisconsin. "I took Bill along and, boy, did they ever enjoy hearing about him! For me, it was a fun afternoon, to say the least."

(We received an interesting question in a letter from an activity director at a nursing home in Kansas after she'd read about Bill Bird-in-Hand in *Birds & Blooms*: "Would this work if Bill was in a *sitting* position?" she asked. "If so, this could prove fascinating and occupy a lot of time for some of our wheelchair guests." After reading that letter, we decided to give it a try. You'll read about those tests in Chapter 11.)

We Kept Hearing "It Worked!"

Our success rate with this test by our Field Editors was incredible. Far, far better than we'd anticipated.

After all, we'd gotten these prototypes out a lot later than we'd hoped—in late March and early April, hardly the best time to entice birds to hand-feed. (As John Leeser said in his early report, "The colder the weather, the better your chances.")

Of the 20 Field Editors on our test team (plus bird authority Hugh Wiberg, whom we added later), *11 were successful* in getting birds to eat out of their hand in short order!

Actually, the percentage was even better than that. Tragically, a fatal accident involving the married daughter of one of the Field Editors understandably canceled the project at their house.

In another case, a Field Editor had agreed to participate in the test, but after receiving our prototype, a job change and move prevented him from getting involved after all.

So all in all, *we had success in 11 of 19 tests!* What's more, most of the remaining eight contend they'll still come through—some of them had to put the project "on hold" due to weather, family or travel reasons and are confident they'll be giving us a positive report soon.

Meet the "Success Team"

Here are the names and hometowns of those 11 people among our test group who had quick success with Bill Bird-in-Hand:

Philip Ahrens, Huntingburg, Indiana…Carolyn Barker, El Reno, Oklahoma…Barbara Dunn, Hollidaysburg, Pennsylvania…Bryan Flagg, Warren, New Hampshire…Sue Gronholz, Beaver Dam, Wisconsin…Diane Heeney, Yankton, South Dakota…Roland Jordahl, Pelican Rapids, Minnesota…Lillian Marcotte, Harland, Vermont…Liz McCain, Florence, Oregon…John Leeser, Macungie, Pennsylvania…and Hugh Wiberg, Wilmington, Massachussetts.

One of the things we heard from these Field Editors is how much they appreciated the "ancillary" benefits of testing Bill:

"The nice thing about Bill is that all of the birds in our backyard have become tamer," said Carolyn Barker of El Reno, Oklahoma. (We heard that comment often from other testers as well.) "The birds come much closer to us now. I guess it's because they're used to having a 'human' among them!

"They're all real comfortable with him. I've seen grackles, mockingbirds, house finches, chickadees and other birds come to his hand.

"It's just so much fun to watch him and the activity around him," continued Carolyn, citing a bit of the fun she's had with her prototype. "We put one of my husband's old hats on Bill, and when our neighbor saw that hat over the fence, he began hollering at my husband but couldn't get him to answer. He was so confused!"

> *"Bill's the best conversation piece I've ever seen..."*

Some of the testers enjoyed proving their spouses and friends wrong. For example, Phil Ahrens of Huntingburg, Indiana wrote, "Within an hour, I had a titmouse eating from my hand. My wife couldn't believe it! She thought there was *no way* that a bird was going to believe I was Bill when I switched places with him."

Phil enjoyed "putting it to" his neighbors as well. "I've had a chance to show off to my neighbors at least a half dozen times. They saw that 'dummy' out in my yard and thought it would never work. But I proved them wrong!"

Testers Did Some "Pioneering"

While our test team was very diligent about following our directions, some of them couldn't resist trying a few novel ideas of their own. One of these was Bryan Flagg of Warren, New Hampshire.

You'll note by Bryan's picture (at right), that instead of *removing* Bill Bird-in-Hand as we suggested, Bryan stepped next to Bill, put his arm around the back of him and his hand right next to Bill's.

And guess who took the picture when that chickadee landed on Bryan's hand—Bryan did. Here's how:

"It was a cloudy, windy, cool day here in New Hampshire. I set up the camera and tripod on my deck, then picked out a spot in front of an apple tree in our front yard to set up good ol' Bill, near two of my feeders.

"Now, here's how quickly I had success: With Bill in place at 11 a.m., I went up on the deck to adjust and focus my camera on him.

"I was amazed—by 11:07, the first chickadee had already landed on Bill's hand. (I snapped the photo.) Then another chickadee swooped in and another sat on his shoulder. (I captured that on film, too.)

"I thought, this is starting off great! Okay, again playing against the odds, at 11:15, I picked up my camera and tripod and set up just in front of Bill…close enough so I could

JOINT EFFORT. Bryan Flagg "broke the rules" but still had success. He put his arm around Bill, and when a chickadee landed on his hand, he shot his own picture.

reach and use the manual release cord. Now I'm all set to go. I thought it would be great to get a picture of Bill and me together. So I put a little seed in my hand and, rather impulsively, put my arm around Bill (he didn't seem to mind much).

"*At 11:26, I had a chickadee on my hand!* I tripped the shutter and can provide photo evidence of that thrilling moment!"

With that kind of quick success "his way", Bryan decided to try it "our way". He removed Bill, put him in the barn, than hurried back to stand in Bill's position in the same pose.

"It was now 11:38 a.m., and although it was somewhat difficult to stand still with seed in one hand and my camera cord in the other, I stood like a statue. At 11:45, a chickadee landed on my hand!

"Those little birds are very quick, and not wanting to miss him, I took the photo just a bit too soon—you'll see that he's just getting ready to land on my hand (at right).

> *"Bill's sort of become a member of our family..."*

"Another landed on my hand not a minute later, and when I tried to take a picture, I found my odds had run out. I was out of film! Then it started raining, and my testing was over for the day."

He Has a Good Sense of Humor

Bryan's reports are fun to read because flashes of his humor keep showing through.

"Bill and I have become pretty good friends over the past month. He doesn't take up much room, and he certainly doesn't eat much. I'm sure the two of us will have many more exciting bird tales to tell in the future," Bryan wrote.

"As for my testing, I know I went against the rules a bit. When I first read over your directions and tips, I said to myself, 'Self, everyone is going to be testing this exactly as they're instructed. As usual, I'll be a little different.'

"So even though I did it a *bit* different than you suggested, I can attest that this project was a true success. In less than *1 hour*, I had birds eating from the palm of my hand.

"I'm not saying that *everyone* will be able to have birds in their hand in under an hour with this method, nor should everyone break the rules as I did. But if this can happen in less

BRYAN SANS BILL. After Bryan Flagg got birds "trained", they came to him regularly.

than an hour when I did it a bit *wrong*, imagine what could happen when people do it *right*.

"What a great experience! It's one I wish all mankind could be privy to. My hats off to the *Birds & Blooms* staff for another successful project. I can't wait for the next one!

"In fact, I have a new idea of my own: I'm going to try to use Bill with hummingbirds. I'll put a small hummingbird feeder on Bill's hand, and then take his place over time. It would be a great thrill to have a hummer eat from a feeder I'm holding in my hand.

"As you can see, I love nature and wildlife. That's the main reason I chose to live in the White Mountains of New Hamp-

SHE DID IT AGAIN. While Barbara Dunn is in the same position here as at the beginning of this chapter, note that this time it's a *male* American goldfinch having a treat. Like other testers, once Barbara met with success, birds kept coming and going.

shire. Projects like Bill Bird-in-Hand can bring people a lot closer to the beauty of nature, and I thank you folks for giving so many people that opportunity."

I guess you can see why we like Bryan...as well as all the other Field Editors who served as part of our test team. They readily volunteered and put in considerable time and effort to make this project credible.

Without them, and without their success, we wouldn't be offering Bill Bird-in-Hand now and making this kind of experience, to "hold a bit of heaven in the palm of their hand", available to thousands of bird enthusiasts across the country.

CHAPTER 9

Thrills Amateurs and Experts Alike

THE THRILL of having a bird alight on your hand isn't diminished or enhanced by age. It appears to have the same awesome effect on everyone.

Young and old, amateurs and experts experience the same excitement when they feel the feet of a feathered creature on their bare skin and only an arm's length away.

Everyone who experiences this for the first time seems to comment on how *light* the bird is. "It weighed no more than a cotton ball," one Bill Bird-in-Hand tester told us. (I've now experienced this myself, and fully agree.)

But when a bird lands on the hand of a child, the thrill is double—the first thrill is that of the child, the second is that of the parent or grandparent who sees the child's reaction.

> *"Can't believe how light the bird was on my hand… it weighed no more than a cotton ball."*

"Our 12-year-old daughter, Heather, has been incorporating this experiment with her 4-H bird-watching project," explained Sue Gronholz of Beaver Dam, Wisconsin. "She and I have really had a lot of fun testing Bill.

"She had success on her second attempt. What a *thrill* that was for her! (And me, too.)"

11-Year-Old Has Quick Success

We received a similar report from Field Editor Lillian Marcotte of Hartland, Vermont. "My grandson, Donald, helped me assemble Bill. While the assembly went well, standing him up proved difficult at first because the ground was frozen." (Editor's Note: See "Staking It Out" on page 61 for suggestions on how to deal with frozen ground.)

"But once we got him up, the fun began," Lillian continued. "We positioned Bill about 20 feet away from my feeders. The birds weren't bothered by Bill at all; they kept eating from the feeders, so we kept moving him closer, just as you suggested.

"After a few days, we had him about 5 feet from the feeder and put some feed in Bill's hand. A few birds perched on his shoulder, but they didn't eat from his hand, so we finally moved him 2-1/2 feet away from the feeder.

> ### Bird Bit
> Most birds prefer water in a birdbath to be no more than 2-1/2 inches deep.

"That was much better," Lillian went on. "More birds rested on his shoulder, and after several days, I saw the first bird go to his hand and take a seed. Much to my surprise, that first bird was a male purple finch.

"A few days later, chickadees showed up, but not as fast I had hoped. I think this was partly because this was their nesting time and they were busy elsewhere.

"The chickadees then started coming pretty regularly, so I covered one feeder and brought in the other. Now the birds *had* to eat out of Bill's hand, and they did it pretty regularly.

"Then one day after school, Ada, my 11-year-old granddaughter, just went out there with a cap on her head and some seeds in her hand and stood right next to Bill—we didn't even take him away.

"In no time at all, a chickadee landed on her hand! She was *thrilled*! That little fellow came back twice for a snack from her hand. I'm sure she'll remember this experience for the rest of her life."

Now It Was Her Turn

Lillian says they have a lot of birds of all different types in her area. "We live at the top of a hill, and I see the New Hampshire mountains from my kitchen window, so wind was a bit of problem now and then for Bill. I drove two strong sticks in the ground behind him, and that kept him steady.

> *"I'm sure my granddaughter will remember this the rest of her life."*

"The birds became very accustomed to him. We sometimes have as many as four or five rose-breasted grosbeaks here at one time—and they eat from Bill's hand, too.

"My one hope is that I can get one of those grosbeaks to eat from my hand—they're such beautiful birds and it would really be something to be that close to one.

"I can't tell you what a joy this has been for me and our children. Thank you for the privilege of taking part in your Bill Bird-in-Hand test."

Lillian, as well as Sue Gronholz, the Wisconsin tester,

"LIKE A 'SPOT' OF SEED?" Before John Leeser's students put seed in their hands, the youngsters sometimes first put seed in a cup. In this case it convinced a tufted titmouse to be a "taker". Several days later, the students put the seed in their hand.

noticed that after having Bill posted near their feeders for some time, that the birds became "tamer".

"I can tell that the birds aren't as shy anymore," Sue said. "They come a lot closer to us now when we're in the yard."

Sue, too, commented on how much fun her family has had with Bill. "First of all, Highway 33 has been detoured, which has resulted in a lot more traffic on our road. And since Bill resides in our front yard, we have had LOTS of comments about 'that man'! It's almost as much fun to watch the reactions of passersby as it is to watch the birds."

The Birds Outsmarted Them

As Sue mentioned at the beginning of this chapter, her daughter Heather was successful on her *second* attempt. "I want to share what happened on Heather's first bird-feeding attempt," she said. "We had a good laugh about it."

Sue explained that her family feeds from four separate feeders plus a suet feeder. "So when Heather was ready to replace Bill the first time, we took down the feeders and put them on the porch steps, not dreaming that the birds would see them.

"Well, shortly after Heather was out there, standing still and posing like Bill, the goldfinches had found the thistle feeder, the downy was at the suet and the juncos were eating the seed near her feet, just as they'd eaten near Bill's feet each day!

"And then there were the chickadees. The little stinkers sat in the bush behind Heather, looked her over good and started eyeing the feeders on the steps. Then they flew to the feeders and ate there. They outsmarted us.

"So the next night, we put the feeders *inside* the porch, and that's when Heather was quickly successful. She was out there for about 45 minutes, and it was hard for her to keep a straight face as the birds came and flitted about her.

"She was really excited, and it was cute watching her. Her face said it all—she was grinning from ear to ear. She thought

76

it was the neatest thing that ever happened to her! The pictures didn't turn out as good as I'd hoped, but Heather and I will have that memory for a long time just the same."

Impressed by Bill's Durability

Field Editor Marlene Condon, our tester in Crozet, Virginia, hadn't had success with her tests as yet but was enthused about the project just the same.

"I set Bill pretty close to my tray feeder right away and noticed small birds—such as juncos and pine siskins—showed no hesitancy about going to the tray with Bill only inches away. However, a blue jay flew to the feeder and was startled by Bill's presence and immediately flew away.

"This occured three times within a few minutes. But in about 15 minutes, there were two blue jays at the feeder.

"From this I learned several things: Bill looked enough like a human that it caused the large birds some concern. I felt this was good; it should make them less concerned when I finally replace him.

"Also, I learned that while larger birds may be wary at first, they quickly get over it. And I concluded that small birds are much bolder and not so worried about an apparent human presence in the vicinity."

Marlene then put seed in Bill's hand, and just 2 days later, she saw pine siskins perching on Bill's head and shoulders, then eating the seed in his hand.

"I'm certain that the birds were ready to eat from my hand

BILL GIVES 'EM A HAND. A common redpoll stops to snack off of Bill's hand in this close-up. While all kinds of birds are drawn to him, chickadees and nuthatches are the easiest ones to "train" when the switch is made from Bill to a person's hand.

if I'd taken Bill's place, but then the weather turned really bad, and I haven't as yet had a chance to replace him as this is being written to meet your deadline."

Marlene was particularly impressed with Bill's durability in the rain—he's made from corrugated plastic, making him virtually weatherproof. "Raccoons are a real problem here and I was worried about them damaging him, but I didn't have any problems with them.

"Bill is pretty well made," she concluded. "In fact, I think he'll keep through many seasons. I plan to store him in the basement during the summer and use him only in the cold months, when birds are more likely to frequent our feeders."

Experts tend to agree with that—the colder the better your chances. Speaking of experts, in the next chapter, you're about to read about the experience of one of the nation's most highly regarded bird-feeding authorities.

CHAPTER 10

Diary of a Bird Expert About Bill

IF YOU DOUBT there's much interest in feeding birds by hand, consider this experience of Hugh Wiberg of Wilmington, Massachusetts:

Last fall, Hugh was asked to speak at an outdoor show in New England about his personal experiences of training birds to eat from his hand.

The sponsors knew Hugh had written a book on the subject. But they didn't know how much interest there would be from people attending the show.

Obviously.

They reserved a room for around 50 people, maybe a few more. But nearly *200* tried to cram in. When they ran out of chairs, it was standing room only.

What's more, producers of the *Martha Stewart Living* TV

A REAL PRO. Hugh Wiberg has been feeding birds from his hand like this for years. He's written a book about his methods, has appeared on Martha Stewart's show and speaks on the topic. Here he hosts a chickadee; on the next page, a nuthatch.

show heard about Hugh and invited him to appear on the show. The resulting program received an incredible response when he demonstrated "live" his step-by-step guide to hand-feeding.

This is just one more indication of how folks across America are "turning to nature". Gardening is now America's No. 1 hobby, quickly and impressively passing any other type of "spare time" activity.

And bird feeding is gaining fast. One marketing study showed that more than *80 million* people in the United States bought birdseed last year! Isn't that incredible?

Talk about a serious hobby! People in sales always say it's one thing to *talk* about an interest, but it's another thing for them to *put money behind it.* So these 80 million people aren't just "talking" about their love for birds—they're spending money to feed birds and bring them to their backyard.

An Expert Tries It Bill's Way

As I mentioned in Chapter 4, we got acquainted last fall with Hugh shortly after he'd written his book, *Hand-Feeding Backyard Birds.*

He sent me a copy for review, and I spent an entire evening reading it from cover to cover. I found it *fascinating.* (If you'd like a copy for yourself, it's available for $19.95 from Storey Books, Schoolhouse Road, Pownal VT 05261; 1-800/441-5700.)

"I remember the first time I watched a chickadee fly down from a tree and perch on someone's hand," Hugh says in the book. "Although that happened more than 20 years ago, it was a special moment that will stay with me forever."

> *"If we can help thousands of people experience a bird on their hand, it doesn't matter what method they use…"*

It wasn't long after that first experience before Hugh was enticing birds to his own hand, and he's been hand-feeding birds ever since. Over the years, he's become regarded as an authority on the subject, which is why we wanted him to try our "Bill Bird-in-Hand method" of getting backyard birds to eat from his hand.

Hugh's book provides a step-by-step guide to training birds the "traditional way". While very effective, it requires a considerable amount of time and patience…far more than the average person might have.

His Way Took Eight Weekends

For instance, in the example Hugh cites in his book, he describes how—the first time he decided to attempt this—he spent Saturday and Sunday mornings in the backyard of his home. He did this on three consecutive weekends, standing near a maple tree about 15 feet from his feeder. He spent 20 to 30 minutes in this position each time.

On the fourth Saturday, he moved five paces closer to the feeder and stood "still as a statue". On each Saturday thereafter, he closed the gap by a foot or two.

By the sixth Saturday, when he was standing only 4 feet away, chickadees continued to come to the feeder without hesitation. On the eighth weekend, they finally ate from his hand.

Knowing Hugh, he probably didn't feel this was too time-consuming. And many other bird enthusiasts might feel the same way.

Bird Bit

A 170-pound man would have to eat 340 pounds of potatoes in a day to compare to the amount of food a ruby-throated hummingbird consumes in 24 hours.

Like Hugh, they probably would enjoy those repeated 20-minute or half-hour "training sessions". After all, they're outdoors…they're near their bird feeders…and they have the scents and sounds of their backyard around them. They probably find this quiet time very relaxing.

Anyone who feels the same way is welcome to get Hugh's book and train birds that way. Quite honestly, the odds of success with that traditional method are likely as good as what they may be with our Bill Bird-in-Hand approach. The question is whether you're willing to spend that much *time*.

When I first described my "shortcut" approach to Hugh, he eagerly asked if he could have one of the Bill prototypes to test for himself. I thought this was very generous of him; after all, the thought crossed my mind that if our tests with Bill were hugely successful, people might be more prone to buy our prototypes than buy his book.

But it was obvious this wasn't a concern for Hugh. For

one, I think he recognized that we would be interested in offering his book to our *Birds & Blooms* readers (which we've already done in this book and in other promotions) so people would have a *choice* of methods.

Secondly, it became apparent in our discussions that he was coming from the same place we are—it doesn't really matter which book or which method people use to train birds to eat from their hand, as long as they end up having the thrill of that personal experience.

Likely, at present, there isn't more than one person in every million who has experienced the excitement of a bird sitting on their hand. (I can't forget that comment of one tester, "I could feel her feet and the warmth of her belly on my hand…it was *awesome!*")

If our efforts or Hugh's efforts can bring that kind of memorable delight to *thousands* of bird enthusiasts and small chil-

dren as well, then we're fully satisfied with what we've collectively achieved.

The Diary, Day by Day

Hugh took a "scientific" approach and purposely tested our method in a different area, where birds were unfamiliar with hand-feeding. He'd been doing his experiments and the photography for his book in parks and bird sanctuaries elsewhere.

"That's absolutely the case," he wrote. "*None* of the birds in my yard had been previously 'conditioned' to hand-feeding before I started

> *"Birds don't appear to be bothered a bit by Bill being closer..."*

this approach with your Bill prototype. This was virgin territory. It had been 8 or 9 years ago since I did some hand-feeding in my yard; by now that was several bird generations ago."

Predictably, having become more "research-oriented" over the years than most of our *Birds & Blooms* Field Editors, Hugh took a more formal approach to his report. It was in diary form, just as he had apparently recorded the day-by-day events for himself after he began his test of Bill Bird-in-Hand on March 24, 2000.

He also took pictures from time to time, and each of those had the exact date and time recorded on the back. Here is his diary verbatim as we received it:

Friday, 3/24: Package containing Bill prototype arrived at my home in Wilmington.

Saturday, 3/25: Got Bill assembled. Time to put together—20 minutes.

Sunday, 3/26: Took down all feeders (five) except one. Put Bill in place about 15 feet from the one remaining sunflower feeder.

Monday, 3/27: No seed in Bill's hand. Birds appear obliv-

84

ious to Bill. They continue eating at feeder.

Tuesday, 3/28: No change. Birds keep coming and going to this one remaining feeder.

Wednesday, 3/29: Moved Bill closer, 8 feet from feeder.

Thursday, 3/30: Birds don't appear to be bothered a bit by Bill being closer.

Friday, 3/31: Moved Bill to within 2 feet of the feeder. Still no seed in Bill's hand.

Saturday, 4/1: No change. Birds still busily eating from feeder.

Sunday, 4/2: Moved Bill right up to the feeder. Put sunflower seed in Bill's hand for first time. After 1-1/2 hours, observed first chickadee land on Bill's hand and take a seed. (Seed still in the feeder as well.)

Monday, 4/3: Watched two chickadees land on Bill's hand, taking seeds. Meanwhile, other species—nuthatches, goldfinches, titmice—continued to take seed only from the feeder.

Tuesday, 4/4: Process slowed noticeably by inclement weather. Rainy and very windy. Wind blew most of the seed out of Bill's hand within 10 to 15 minutes. Birds kept coming to the feeder.

Wednesday, 4/5: More of same. Very windy. Suggestion: Consider fashioning a 1/2-inch "lip" around the inside of the seed opening on Bill's hand. This should help keep seeds from blowing out. (Editor's Note: We've dealt with this by making the recessed area of Bill's hand deeper.)

Thursday, 4/6: Wind subsiding. Seed now staying in Bill's hand. Sporadic landings on Bill, but by chickadees only.

Friday, 4/7: Removed the feeder from next to Bill (all others had been removed at the start of experiment). Bill now stands alone.

Saturday, 4/8: More bad weather. Rain and 30- to 40-mph wind gusts. Replaced seed several times on Bill's hand. Chickadees now being joined on Bill's hand by goldfinches.

Bill needed more stability to handle these wind problems. Solved the problem by driving 16-inch stakes halfway into ground in front and in back of Bill's feet, snug up against Bill's legs. (See photo at right.)

Sunday, 4/9: More rain in the a.m. Still windy, but saw first titmouse on Bill's hand along with four or five chickadees and several goldfinches. (In heavy downpours, I'd suggest bringing Bill inside, even though Bill is well constructed and appears to weather dampness and strong winds quite well.)

Monday, 4/10: Continuation of birds becoming more comfortable with Bill as their only remaining seed source. Several species are now eating from his hand regularly.

Tuesday, 4/11: Four species now coming and going regularly to Bill. I know the "instructions" say to remove Bill entirely and then stand in his place, but early this morning I stood beside Bill for 30 minutes. No takers. Birds continued to come to Bill's hand, but not to mine.

Wednesday, 4/12: More of same, less windy. More and more bird activity on Bill.

Thursday, 4/13: At daybreak, I removed Bill entirely. (Now playing by the "rules".) Watched from the house for an hour as birds flitted around, looking for Bill.

I then went outside with seed in my hand, standing exactly where Bill was and in the exact position.

In 10 minutes, a chickadee landed on my hand! It came back twice almost immediately. The concept works!

Feels "Bill" Will Be a Hero

I felt this unique method would work before I started the process, but this confirmed it. Bill had done all the waiting for me. And in only 10 minutes the first time I took his place, I had a bird on my hand!

I'm confident that other species will come to my hand within a day or two, but I know you're waiting for this report to meet your deadline, so I'm putting it in the mail.

Congratulations on a unique, time-saving concept! With this new approach or the traditional approach, you sometimes have to be as lucky as you are good, because weather and animals may come into play.

I am sure of this: You'll have a higher rate of success and quicker results in winter than with the test I just completed in late March and early April. That's because at this time of year, birds are more concerned about mating and sitting on

> *"In 10 minutes, a chickadee landed on my hand! The concept works!"*

eggs. Training birds to eat from your hand is much easier when the weather is cold and food is hard to find.

Again, I am absolutely convinced that your Bill Bird-in-Hand concept works. In my opinion, Bill could become a real backyard "hero" across the country. Who else would be willing to do all the standing, waiting and "training" for thousands of people too busy to do it on their own…in order to give each of them the unmatchable thrill of having a bird eat from their hands?

Unexpected Benefits of Bill

ONE of the Field Editors who helped us test Bill reflected on the experience and discovered these benefits:

- The opportunity for close observation of a great variety of birds in your backyard.
- A chance to observe bird behavior and how it differs between species.
- The opportunity to develop your listening skills by being aware of the many different bird calls and who they belong to.
- Watching nature unfold, especially during the early morning hours—seeing the heavily laden dewdrops on flowers and plants slowly evaporate as the morning sun hits them…and noticing a gentle breeze carrying flower fragrances through your backyard.
- Enjoying the time this experiment offers you to relax and meditate, whether you have success or not.
- Learning a lesson in *patience*. In today's hectic society, we could all use a lesson in that. Interestingly, in my case, it was taught by a "dummy" named Bill.

CHAPTER 11

When Bill Sat Down on the Job

"IN your most recent issue of *Birds & Blooms*, the article about Bill Bird-in-Hand caught my attention," the letter began. "At first, I thought how wonderful it would be to have birds in my own yard eating out of my hand.

"Then I realized that there are others who would derive a great deal of joy from it also. You see, I work in a nursing home. Our beloved residents are limited in so many ways. I cannot describe the joy their faces would express to have a little bird eating from their hand."

The letter was from Tina Cole of Montezuma, Kansas. "Would it be possible for you to develop a handicapped-accessible Bill?" she continued. "If he could be *seated*, for example, a person in a wheelchair could be substituted for him and have the opportunity to experience

> *"Our nursing home residents would love to give him a try if you could make him work at wheelchair level..."*

the excitement of feeding birds from his or her hand. I'm sure our residents would *love* to give him a try."

Tina's letter got us thinking. If we could make Bill work in a *sitting* position, just picture the fascinating activity this could offer *thousands* of people in nursing homes and senior centers!

For example, if one of our Bills was set up just outside their lounge or dining area, think of the conversations that would spark among those people. They'd have something *new* to talk about...it would be a project they all could get *involved* in...it would give a boost to their camaraderie and make them feel they were working on the project *together*.

89

It would give them something to *look forward to* each day as they watched Bill being moved closer and closer to the feeder...and they could *jointly decide* who among them was going to take Bill's place when they were ready for the "switch".

By then, can you imagine the *excitement if and when that first bird ate from that resident's hand?*

That's not all. Think of the continued excitement as other residents took their turn donning Bill's shirt and hat, then sitting in his place.

LOUNGING ABOUT. Some of our testers thought of trying Bill in a sitting position before we did. This one let him relax in a lounge chair!

The chance of success would start all over with each resident. And for these people to have a once-in-a-lifetime experience like this at that age would prove mighty exciting— "Imagine, I had a bird sitting right in my hand!"

Could Bill Sit This One Out?

Other subscribers gave us other reasons to check out the "sitting approach" after we published the article about Bill. For example, here's the point that Natalie Hunter of Athens, Ohio made in her handwritten letter:

"My mother and I saw the Bill Bird-in-Hand training device in your June/July 2000 issue of *Birds & Blooms* and came up with a twist on the idea: Why not make a prototype that can sit in a chair? I would love to have a bird eat from my hand," Natalie continued, "but I simply do not have the patience or the inclination to stand still for even a half hour, much less an hour at a time.

"If Bill could train the birds from a sitting position, I'd be more interested…and I'm sure many of your other subscribers feel the same way.

"I think the response would be overwhelming. I hope you take our idea into consideration."

Well, we did. At the same time, we pointed out in our return letter to Natalie that, when using Bill successfully, you aren't required to stand out there near the feeder an hour or half hour *day after day*. Bill does that for you.

You only stand there for a half hour or so *one time*—if, like many of our testers, you're fortunate to be successful on your first attempt when you switch places with Bill.

Again, this kind of success or any success is not *guaranteed* with the "Bill method" or the "traditional" training method. But, as shared in Chapter 8 of this book, *11* of our *19* test team members did have that kind of quick success.

Rain Nor Sleet Nor Snow...But Wind?

So, we emphasized to Natalie, it doesn't take a lot of "patience" with the Bill Bird-in-Hand method. On the other hand, we had another reason for wanting to know if the sitting approach would work. While the tests showed that Bill is durable enough to withstand rain, snow and sleet, we'd learned that strong winds could sometimes be a problem.

> ## Bird Bit
> The northern cardinal was introduced to Hawaii by homesick Americans from the eastern United States.

We'd designed him in an upright position for good reason. That way, after you've moved Bill closer and closer to your feeder, then finally empty your feeder and put seed in Bill's hand, it will be very close to the level of the feeder tray. When birds find the feeder empty, they quickly spot the nearby feed in Bill's hand.

That's the benefit of having him upright. While a few of our testers in high-wind areas found they had to add extra support to bolster Bill, this didn't prove that difficult for them; they just put several stakes in front and back of Bill (see the example on page 86) or came up with some other approach to make him sturdy.

Still, if Bill could be proven effective in a *sitting* position, wind wouldn't be as much of a problem. Plus, we had a good second reason for concluding the sitting position would be beneficial: If Bill was in a chair, *he would be much easier to move a few feet each day.*

It's a fact that when the ground is frozen, or you're dealing with hard or rocky soil, it can be somewhat difficult to get Bill's support pole in and out of the ground to change his position regularly. Although we and our testers have come up with suggestions to make that easier, too (see "Staking It Out" on page 61), we recognize that moving Bill's chair closer and closer each day would be far easier than repositioning his support pole when he's standing.

Concerned Whether It Works as Well

From a manufacturing standpoint, we knew it would be no problem to convert Bill to a sitting position. It would just be a matter of "scoring" the prototype at the knee level. After all, we were already adding a crease at his waist level, allowing us to fold the prototype in half and ship it in a smaller box.

But we had another concern: Would the *distance* between the height of the feeder tray and Bill's hand be a problem if he was in a sitting position?

As mentioned above, one of the reasons for and benefits of having Bill in a standing position is that when you're ready to empty the feeder and put the seed in his hand, Bill's hand is very close to the same level as the feeder tray and therefore easily noticed by the birds.

Would they be as likely to spot seed in his hand several feet below the feeder tray? Even if they did, would they be as comfortable going to his hand there…as compared to going from the feeder to his hand just several inches away?

Surprise! It Had Already Been Done!

We began digging through all the reports and photos we'd received from our Field Editors who tested Bill and were surprised to find that one of them—Roland Jordahl of Pelican Rapids, Minnesota—*had already had success with Bill in a sitting position.*

He'd even provided photo evidence. We learned he'd tried this on his own because he has back and knee problems. You'll learn all about Roland's experience in the next chapter.

Meantime, we decided to check it out on our own, so we'd have more than one test to confirm the results.

OUR OWN TEST. Here's "sitting Bill" being tested behind a nursing home that's close to our company offices.

We went to a nursing home near our offices and talked to the activity director there. She thought it was a *wonderful* idea and felt sure some of her residents would be more than willing to test the unit for us.

The director also felt that *all* of the residents would be interested in watching the progress of the test as it developed (confirming our earlier hunch that this would be a fascinating activity for any senior center). With her approval, we put up a feeder behind the residence. Surprisingly—to me at least—they didn't have a single bird feeder on the grounds. (I'm admittedly a bird nut, but it seems to me that *every* nursing home or senior center should have one or more bird feeders! Bird-watching is such a simple, satisfying hobby for everyone, especially for seniors who are limited in the other things they're able to do.)

We Gladly Donated a Feeder

Anyway…we set up one of the special "squirrel-proof" feeders offered by our company's Country Store mail-order division. (No squirrel has beaten it yet—it's the one shown in the picture below; see page 121 for more details about it.)

Before we put the feeder's support pole in the ground, though, we cut off about a foot of its length to purposely make it just a little *lower*. We felt that way, when Bill was finally positioned next to it, his hand would be a foot closer to the feeder tray. Then we set Bill in a chair about 30 feet away.

Each day for a week or more, we moved him just a bit closer. These short, daily moves were easy, since all we had to do was move Bill's chair with him in it.

We finally got him right next to the feeder, but our test ran into a problem: We weren't attracting the right kind of birds.

For some reason, there were no chickadees, nuthatches or tufted titmice in that area, even though we have a host of those same birds on our company grounds just a block or two away. While many birds came to the feeder, and continued to come daily as we moved Bill closer, they were all sparrows, mourning doves, blackbirds, grackles and the like.

Those birds aren't as "trainable" as the former three. We left the feeder and Bill in that position an extra week, hoping that the chickadees and their friends would soon find this new seed source. It never happened…which proves that not everyone—even eager bird enthusiasts such as us—will have success *every time* with our method or any method.

So, we finally gave up at that location and moved Bill to my backyard. And for me, *that's when the fun really began!*

You see, I still hadn't been able to give Bill a try on my own. As I mentioned in Chapter 1, we felt this whole experiment would be much more believable if it was conducted by an unbiased person not connected with our company.

That's why we picked John Leeser in Pennsylvania for our initial test. Then, for the same reason, we selected 20 Field Editors for the second round of trials.

Now, finally, with just this one prototype available, I decided it was time to move it from the nursing home to my home (don't read anything into that, okay?). After all the excitement and success I'd heard from these people, I wanted to experience this Bill Bird-in-Hand approach myself.

Bill and I Sat Down on the Job

What made this all the more challenging and exciting for me is that I would personally be able to see if Bill could be made to work in the *sitting* position. Since to date we'd only had a single report of success

> *"I soon wished I hadn't picked a hard metal chair!"*

when Bill sat down on the job, I felt like I was being part of our "research", rather than just repeating the success of others.

So, on a Sunday afternoon, I set up the same feeder near our house, put Bill in one of our lawn chairs, then left him there for a week. Each evening when I came home from work, I moved him a bit closer. I noticed large numbers of house finches in the area, but no chickadees or nuthatches.

By Saturday he was right next to the feeder, so I clamped it shut and put seed in his hand. Early Sunday morning I

found the hand empty, "reloaded" it and went inside to read the paper. Two hours later, it was empty again. I figured the birds were ready.

I removed Bill, hid him behind some trees, put on his shirt and cap, then sat in the chair. I tossed a little seed on the ground in front of me, put a few kernels on top of my cap, my shoulders and on my knees, then held the rest in my hand.

BULGING BILL. Note I put some "padding" inside Bill's shirt to give him more shape, and shortened the feeder support pole. Feeder is clamped shut to focus birds on Bill's hand.

Checked my watch: 11:05 a.m. It took about 10 minutes for the birds to come back. But even after only 10 minutes, my arm got tired. And I wished I hadn't picked a hard metal chair.

Finally, I heard finches peeping on the tree right behind me, and I "made like a statue". Four flew to the ground in front of me and began pecking at the seed I'd tossed there. Two got very close, and one even picked at my shoe. Their coming this close was encouraging: "They must think I'm Bill!"

I felt one of those from the tree behind me land right on top of my cap and start pecking away. Even that was a thrill. I'd never been that close to a wild bird before!

Then something funny happened: He hopped on the bill of my cap, and as he ate I could see his tail twittering right off the edge of the brim. Suddenly, he turned around, leaned over the edge and looked right in my face! *Our eyes were inches apart.* It startled both of us. He burst off so fast my cap dipped down! It was as though he said, "Holy cow, that's not Bill!"

I stayed put, breathing slowly, eyes closed to slits so they couldn't see me blink or my eyes moving. Then it happened. A finch flew so close to my right ear I felt the wind from his wings. He lit on my knee and picked a kernel or two; I could feel his tiny feet on my leg. Then he hopped up to my hand.

Wow, <u>what a thrill</u>! I quickly experienced everything all those Field Editors and others had described. A wild bird was eating from my hand for the first time ever!

And he didn't just take a kernel and fly off. He stayed for at least 2 minutes, nonchalantly enjoying his lunch.

When he finally took off, so did I. I ran for the house to tell Bobbi. Really, I *ran.*

She grabbed her camera and we hurried out to try it again. The first time it had taken me 14 minutes. The second time, it

IT WORKED! This is the first time I've ever experienced a bird on my hand! And it happened in only *14 minutes* from the time that I replaced Bill in the chair. What a *thrill.*

took only *8 minutes.* The bird first landed on my cap (the seed up there proved to be good "bait" to draw them in), then hopped up to my hand. She snapped the photo above.

This was especially satisfying to me, not only because it allowed Bobbi to get some photo evidence, but so that I could have her see firsthand that this wild idea I'd had months before really *worked*. Again, the bird stayed for several minutes.

When it took off, I said, "Okay, let's change places and see if it works for you, too." That was even more amazing.

She was wearing a dress (see below), which hardly looked anything like Bill's "pants". Nevertheless, she slipped on Bill's shirt and cap, filled her hand with seed and sat down.

How Could It Happen That Fast??

I hardly had time to get the camera focused before three finches landed in that tree right behind her. Then one swooped down directly to her hand and started eating!

She hadn't been there *2 minutes*. As she said later, "He stayed longer than it took him to come to my hand!"

That day will always be special for us. It was Sunday, August 6, 2000. It was the first time either of us had ever experienced the thrill of having a wild bird eat from our hands.

Better yet, we'd both accomplished it from a sitting position. This made us confident that thousands of others—including anyone who has difficulty standing for a long period —would be able to enjoy this same *wonderful* experience.

SUCCESS IN *2 MINUTES*. That's all it took for Bobbi to get this finch to eat from her hand on her very first attempt!

COULDN'T CAP IT OFF. Later, when Bobbi tried it without wearing the cap, it didn't work. The birds noticed the difference.

CHAPTER 12

Bad Back Lowers Expectations

WE SHOULDN'T have favorites among the more than 100 Field Editors around the country who contribute to *Birds & Blooms* regularly (they keep us and our readers informed about what's happening bird-wise and flower-wise in their areas). But we will admit that one we especially enjoy hearing from is Roland Jordahl of Pelican Rapids, Minnesota.

You'll see why here and in the pages ahead. Not only does his Norwegian humor keep coming through, but he has interesting viewpoints and is a genuinely sensitive guy.

Evidence of the latter are these recent quotes of Roland's: "It's a really satisfying experience to have a bird land on your hand. It's just very heartwarming and rewarding to feel that such a small creature places such *trust* in you.

> *"I felt I had two strikes against this working... but on the second attempt, I was surprised by a nuthatch!"*

"I'm always amazed at just how *light* these little birds are when they land on your hand. And each time, you sense a special bond between you and wildlife."

Roland's test of Bill Bird-in-Hand didn't start off well. First it was the weather. Then it was his wife. Then it was his back.

Bill Got "Snowed in"

We shipped the Bill prototype to Roland in late March. The first we heard from Roland after that was on April 10. "Thought I'd give you an update on Bill," he wrote. "Would you believe it? Would you really *believe* it if I told you that it is snowing very hard here right now? On *April 10*? Over 5 inches of the pretty stuff.

"Our lawn was green. It's now white. The tulips were 2 inches high; they're now buried under snow. Bill's standing outside with a white angel food cake on his head. (That "cake" is shown in the photo at left.) Uffda, this is tough even for a Norwegian!"

Roland's report described other delays in getting started with his test of Bill.

"On March 25, I put Bill together. I reinforced all of the tabs with 2-inch 3M tape. I *am* from Minnesota.

"I built a special base with two-by-twos and a four-by-four so I could move Bill around a bit easier. (See photo on opposite page.) Then I placed him in the backyard about 30 feet from one of my feeding stations.

"From March 28 to March 30, I moved Bill closer to the feeding station each day," Roland continued. "Strong winds blew so hard, they blew Bill over even when I'd put rocks on the base. This *is* Minnesota.

"On March 29, I added some seed to Bill's hand. Later, I saw one common redpoll sit on Bill's hand.

"March 30, I saw the first chickadee coming to Bill's hand. Things were going well. I was getting ready to close off the feeder, etc. Then it happened.

Backing Off of Bill

"April 1, back problems. (Me, not Bill.) Serious kind. I was laid up for a week. Then my wife was rushed to the hospital and spent some time there. The weather turned sour besides.

"Now, it's April 10 and we've been hit with all this snow and cold. I think we'll have to wait a bit to get this 'experiment' going again. I'm taking him inside."

Ironically, it was that back problem of Roland's that resulted in our first "sitting test". We didn't hear from him again until May 21, long after most of the other members of the test team had reported in.

Started Over in May

"Bill was officially replaced in my yard on the morning of May 19," he wrote. "Temperature was 40°, very windy, but the sun was shining.

"I realize this is not a good time to start a hand-feeding project like this. Birds are already breeding and nesting and have so much natural food available that they don't have as much incentive to come to a 'questionable hand' for food.

"I know this would work much better in fall, winter and early spring. But I'm eager to give it a try now and am going ahead."

Since the birds in his yard had seen Bill back in April, Roland started with Bill pretty close to the feeder this time. (See at right.) And he closed off the other feeders to have them concentrate on the one near Bill.

Against the Odds

"In a way, I felt I had two strikes against this working," Roland admitted. "First of all, it was now getting quite late in the season for this. And secondly, due to my back problems and a knee problem besides, I couldn't stand out there

SAME BILL, BETTER WEATHER. When Roland finally put Bill back out in his yard in May, he started with him closer to his feeder.

next to him for any length of time. So, when I was ready to switch places with Bill, I sat in a chair. (See photo below.) You'll note I put on the same shirt and hat as Bill had been wearing. I was ready for action.

"This was on May 21, only 2 days after I'd put Bill back in his old position. I'd noticed that the birds seemed comfortable with him right away, and I was in a hurry, so I changed positions with him rather hurriedly.

READY AND WAITING. Roland Jordahl takes Bill's place in the chair, with seed in one hand and his camera remote release in the other.

"I prepared in advance by setting up my camera on a tripod, then held the seed in one hand and the remote control for the camera in the other, so I could snap off a photo if I had any luck.

"I didn't. Not that first day. But I enjoyed the experience just the same. While none of them landed on my hand, I had birds within 6 to 10 feet of me, including red-bellied woodpeckers, chipping sparrows, downy woodpeckers, black-capped chickadees, white-breasted nuthatches, mourning doves, ruby-throated hummingbirds, rose-breasted grosbeaks and red-winged blackbirds.

Felt Bill Deserved the Credit

"It was wonderful to observe that variety of birds up close. And I'm sure it was Bill who had made them comfortable with that while he sat out there for days in my yard. There was a humorous moment, too, that lightened the morning. While I was sitting there with all those birds flying around me, a chickadee landed on my camera on the tripod. From there he cocked his head and *stared* at me as though he was studying what I was doing. Then he fluttered off, looking very perplexed.

"Still, while I enjoyed that and the other wildlife experiences out there, I began to doubt my chances of success. There was a considerable difference in height between what the birds had been used to at the feeder and the height of my hand from a sitting position. I wondered if they would ever come down to my level.

"After nearly an hour that first time, I decided to try another day. Had other things to do. So for that first day, it was 'Birds 1, Roland 0'.

"I went right back out the next day, on May 22,

SUCCESS! Just as he was thinking about giving up, a white-breasted nuthatch landed, and Roland snapped this picture of himself.

and sat in the chair again. This time I had on the *Birds & Blooms* shirt that the *B&B* staff was kind enough to send to me. (Maybe it brought good luck.)

"I held seed in my hand, rested my arm on the chair and held the camera remote in the other hand again, even though I wasn't expecting much. I should have. In about 25 minutes, a white-breasted nuthatch descended out of nowhere and *landed on my feeding hand*! (See photo on page 103.)

"He sorted through the seeds, picking out the one he wanted, and stayed long enough for me to snap off four pictures with my remote. *So I had success from a sitting position and knew I had the photo evidence to prove it!*

"That happened just this morning, and I'm sure I'll have continued success, but I know you're waiting for this report, so I'm dashing it off and getting it in the mail to you."

Birds Were Able to Adapt

What we found particularly interesting in Roland's case is that he had "trained" his birds with Bill in the standing position...then, when he traded places with Bill, he had success in drawing them to his own hand while in a sitting position.

This seems to indicate that once birds become acclimated to the regular presence of a "person" near the seed source, they're comfortable no matter how a human replaces Bill and will look for food anywhere nearby. It could take longer to draw them in this way, but on the other hand, the wait is easier. After all, you're *sitting* rather than standing.

"THANKS, BILL!" Roland Jordahl thanked Bill for "enduring many hours of standing in for me through wind, rain and snow"...and added, "Bill has become part of the family."

CHAPTER 13

Bill's Gone! Call the Cops!

OUR GROUP of *Birds & Blooms* Field Editors who tested Bill Bird-in-Hand had some highly interesting and enjoyable experiences. You'll read some of the highlights they shared with us in the pages ahead.

Probably the most surprising thing that happened was in Charles City, Iowa, where our Bill prototype was *abducted* from our tester's front yard one night. To make matters all the more exciting, the local police put out an "APB" on Bill!

We're quite sure they did that to have a little fun. But it seems only proper that the All Points Bulletin for a missing person should have reported it as a "Bill-napping".

Wendell Obermeier, our Field Editor/test team member in Charles City who was the "victim" of the theft, was interviewed by a staff writer of the *Charles City Press* about the incident. Soon everybody in town was talking about it, Wendell told us.

> *"You just can't believe the uproar Bill's abduction has caused around here!"*

"You just can't believe the uproar Bill's abduction and the resulting publicity has caused! Everywhere we go it is the topic of conversation—at church, the barbershop, the beauty parlor and even at the local hospital," Wendell related.

"We've gotten a lot of phone calls about it. And last night at the cafe where we were eating, almost everyone who passed our table stopped to visit about Bill and why anyone would steal him."

Even the minister at the Obermeiers' church got in on the fun. While they were attending a family breakfast there, the minister came up and said, "Obie, I think I know what happened. One of the sports bars in town has had a cardboard girl outside, and she's missing, too. I think Bill and that gal ran off together!"

To date, there's been no trace of the missing prototype, and Bill continues to be a popular topic of conversations in Charles City. In fact, Wendell shared this wincer: "We attended a funeral last Thursday, and the conversation was more about Bill than the deceased!"

HE SUBSCRIBES? Testers had all sorts of fun with Bill. Carolyn Barker had people believing Bill could read!

Other Field Editors involved in testing Bill reported they'd received a lot of attention from both neighbors and passersby.

"I've really enjoyed having him around," commented Carolyn Barker of El Reno, Oklahoma. "He's just fun to watch.

Put Bill in the Passenger Seat?

"I often see birds land on his head and check him out. I've had grackles, mockingbirds, house finches and chickadees all come to his hand. I was originally afraid he would prevent orioles and hummingbirds from coming in my yard, but that hasn't been the case."

Then Carolyn jokingly added, "Bill's gotten so much attention around here, I'm planning to take him for a car ride someday so everyone thinks I have a boyfriend!"

As you can see by the picture on the opposite page, Carolyn has already had some fun with Bill. She posed him at her kitchen table, reading *Birds & Blooms* no less, to surprise a friend who came to visit.

Herb Schmid of Big Bear City, California had fun with his prototype, too. After his wife took a digital picture of Herb's face, Herb enlarged it on his computer to be the same size as the face on Bill Bird-in-Hand.

Pasted in place, the face on his Bill now looks exactly like Herb. So much so, in fact, that when his son-in-law came to visit, he glanced at the "dummy" near the porch and said, "Hi, Dad." When he didn't get an answer, he investigated more closely and had a good laugh.

Bill Draws Birds in Closer

Kathy Justy of Grafton, Ohio noticed the same thing as many of the other testers. "The birds in my yard are tamer since I've had Bill out there," she said. "They all seem to trust me more now. The other day I had nuthatches just 2 feet

WHERE'S BILL? Oh, there he is. Field Editors tested Bill all over, even in the woods.

away from me, and I realized it was likely because I had a hat on that was similar to Bill's."

After Kathy got birds to eat seed from Bill's hand, she placed a hummingbird feeder in his hand. Both hummers and orioles were soon coming to the feeder at the time of her report, and she was getting ready to switch with Bill to see if they would drink while she held it instead! (We'll report the result of this test and other ongoing experiments by our Field Editors in future issues of *Birds & Blooms*.)

She Succeeded Without Bill!

Normally, if someone was selling something, they likely wouldn't tell people how they can get along without it. But, as

HID BEHIND TREE. Danette Manes of Spirit Lake, Idaho came up with an unusual way of getting this chickadee to eat from her hand, as you'll learn at right.

I said in Chapter 10, it doesn't really matter to me which method people use to train birds to eat from their hand, as long as they end up having the thrill of that personal experience.

Therefore, I wasn't bothered at all by the letter and photos from Danette Manes of Spirit Lake, Idaho, who had read about our hand-feeding experiments in *Birds & Blooms*, then came up with her own method of making the approach work...without Bill.

"After unsuccessfully trying to hand-feed birds for several years, I was inspired by your Bill Bird-in-Hand article," Danette hand-penned.

"After reading that article

FAMILY AFFAIR. Same chickadee was hand-fed by everyone in Manes family.

closely, I decided to put our platform feeder right up against a tree," she continued. "Then I hid behind the tree, put feed in my hand and held my hand out over the platform feeder.

"It worked! A mountain chickadee was making trips to the feeder, and it wasn't long before she was *perching on my* hand, gathering up food for the five babies that I soon found she had in a nest nearby."

Bird Befriended Whole Family

Danette removed the platform feeder and gradually moved out from behind the tree. The little bird kept coming.

"My husband, daughter, son and I hand-fed this chickadee twice a day for about 2 weeks," Danette relates. "She became so tame that eventually all we had to do was walk out our door and hold out a hand, and she would come to perch on it, whether we had seed on it or not.

"One day my husband was outside talking to a friend when our little chickadee flew up and landed on his head! This little bird brought us so much pleasure and joy.

"I could even put feed on my shoulder and she would perch there. My daughter Angie tried to pet this chickadee, and she did finally let us gently rub her back or head.

"Her five babies left the nest yesterday and she left with them. We will surely miss her and will always cherish the experience of feeding this little mama bird from our hands.

> ### Bird Bit
> Most people think a white-breasted nuthatch is pecking at a tree in search for grubs. But sometimes he's storing food by tucking it in the crevices of a tree cavity.

"Thanks for a wonderful magazine and for such great birding ideas ...especially this one that led to a monthful of memories for our family!"

This is a heartwarming story. So, if you have a tree in your backyard big enough to hide behind, you may have success with the "Danette method" as well as the "Bill method". On the other hand, if you don't have time to grow a tree that big, Bill still may be your best option.

Do We Need a Female Version?

One of our staffers suggested that, instead of just having a *Bill* Bird-in-Hand, we should consider offering a "Bobbi" Bird-in-Hand as well. (Someone named it "Bobbi" after my wife.) So, during our tests, we took a picture of one of our female editors, enlarged it and replaced Bill's with it.

We couldn't tell any difference in the response. Nor did it make any difference when a man or woman changed places with it.

John Leeser's test also proved the birds weren't "gender concious". As evidence, turn back to page 33. You'll see that while he had our Bill do the waiting, on the day he made the switch, his daughter, Jaimie, stood in for Bill. And the birds still came to her hand in less than an hour on her first try.

So, since offering two different versions—male and female prototypes—would substantially increase our costs (and therefore raise the price for buyers), we decided to just go with Bill for now. If we learn later that a great number of our female readers would still prefer a *"Bobbi* Bird-in-Hand", we'll consider it.

In the meantime, users might consider doing what Herb Schmid did. As stated earlier in this chapter, Herb had a picture taken of himself, then enlarged it to the same size as Bill's and pasted it in place.

With today's easy access to photo enlargements, anyone could do the same. The fact that Herb's son-in-law said "Hi, Dad" to the mannequin illustrates just how effective that can be!

Of course, your friends and neighbors may wonder why you're spending all that time standing stiffly in your yard!

"BOBBI BIRD-IN-HAND"? We tested a female version of our Bill prototype, but could see no difference in response. Guess birds aren't "gender conscious".

"WHAT? NO SNACK?" Once birds are trained to come to your hand, they'll often come even when you don't have feed—as this chickadee did—just to check things out.

CHAPTER 14

Does Hand-Feeding Endanger Birds?

THE quick answer: No. Not according to research and the experiences of bird authorities. And they give some good reasons why.

Still, there are some people who indicate concern over the "intrusive" aspect of training birds to hand-feed. These folks fear that taming birds to this point might encourage them to come within reach of people who could harm them.

> *"I wouldn't consider it any more intrusive than setting up a feeder in my backyard..."*

There's no evidence to suggest this is the case. Bird authority Hugh Wiberg, for example (you met him in Chapter 10), has been hand-feeding birds—and teaching others to do it—for more than 20 years. And he has yet to see or hear of a single instance in which a bird that has learned to hand-feed has been threatened or harmed by a human.

A lengthy study by the University of Wisconsin's Department of Wildlife Ecology validated that same conclusion.

Hugh and other authorities make this point: The kind of people who visit wildlife sanctuaries, state parks and other woodland areas are not people who would go out of their way to bring harm to any type of wildlife. These people invariably respect wildlife, including the few birds that have learned to be hand-fed.

In Hugh's book, *Hand-Feeding Backyard Birds*, he tells of contacting 10 professionals in the field of birding, either authors of bird books or people otherwise engaged in some aspect of ornithology. He posed this question to each of them:

NO NEED TO STOP HANDOUTS. Experts find no harm in feeding birds by hand or through handouts, such as the jelly and orange treat this male house finch is enjoying.

"Would you consider hand-feeding wild birds to be harmfully intrusive?" Their replies were unanimous: Hand-feeding does not endanger birds.

What the Experts Say

Said John V. Dennis, author of more than a dozen bird books, "After my many years in the field of ornithology, I would agree that hand-feeding wild birds is not intrusive."

And this is the quote in Hugh's book from Dr. Roger Tory Peterson, who most birders consider to be the world's foremost authority on birds: "Absolutely not, so far as I have observed. I have fed many a chickadee from my hands, as well as nuthatches, titmice and several other birds...I have never seen anyone take unethical advantage of the situation."

Finally, Donald Hyde, president of the Hyde Bird Feeder Company in Waltham, Massachusetts, said: "I would not consider hand-feeding wild birds any more intrusive than setting up a feeder in my backyard."

The University of Wisconsin test went a bit further; it studied whether birds fed at backyard feeders will eventually lose their instinctive abilities to survive. The results were published in the spring 1992 issue of the *Journal of Field Ornithology*.

They Did Just Fine, Thank You

One of the questions addressed by the researchers was, "Will wild birds lose some or all of their natural abilities to survive harsh winters as a result of the generosity of millions of Americans and Canadians who tend bird feeders?"

To learn the answer, two groups of chickadees were monitored over several years. The first group had no possible association with bird feeders...while the second group was fed regularly for

> **Bird Bit**
> Black oil sunflower seeds, a favorite of many songbirds, contain more than 45% oil.

3 years before being suddenly cut off from their bird-feeder handouts.

The two groups were then studied during several following winters. The researchers concluded there was no measurable difference in the rate of survival between the two groups.

Likewise, Hugh has noticed that the birds he was hand-feeding from October to March suffered no ill effects when

April came and he, along with other hand-feeders, stopped hand-feeding for the summer. He was able to conclude this because he came to recognize several birds who came to him—due to their physical differences—and they seemed fit and healthy when they returned to him after a 6-month separation.

Amazingly, those birds still recognized him as the "generous soft touch" after that 6-month lapse! Again, this shows one of the exciting personal benefits of training birds to hand-feed.

YOU COULD GET THIS CLOSE. After teaching birds to eat from your hand, you could get a close-up look at birds like these. As many in the test group pointed out, the steady presence of Bill in their backyard made all types of birds tamer.

CHAPTER 15

Now It's *Your* Turn to Test—and Tell

YOU'VE now read Bill's Story. I've shared with you how the idea for him came about…how we experimented with it on our own…how we had it tested by 18 *Birds & Blooms* Field Editors plus one bird expert…and how then, with quick success on more than half of those tests and my own experience, we applied for a patent and decided to offer our Bill Bird-in-Hand product to bird enthusiasts across the country.

If you haven't already done so, hopefully you will now want to order a Bill for your backyard. As I said in the Foreword, we can't *guarantee* this method will work, any more than advocates of the traditional method can guarantee their long-term approach.

First of all, Bill works best if you have the *right kind* of birds in your backyard. Normally, it's chickadees, nuthatches and tufted titmice that are bold enough to be coaxed to your hand…by the Bill method or any method.

> *"Not knowing whether you'll succeed is part of the 'fun' of this whole process…"*

If you don't have any of those three birds in your area, your chances of success may be slightly reduced. Still, as you now know, some members of our test team and I were able to draw in finches, which are normally quite skittish, as well as downy woodpeckers on our very *first* attempt.

As we pointed out earlier, *not knowing* whether you'll have success is part of the "fun" of this whole process, just as part of the fun of fishing is not knowing whether you'll catch anything. The trial and error, the "I succeeded and you didn't" part of this fascinating experience is also part of the enjoyment. Again, if everyone could get a bird to eat off their hand immediately, on their first try, it wouldn't be such a novel, special experience.

So, while we can't guarantee success with Bill Bird-in-Hand any more than those who sell fishing lures can *guarantee* you'll catch a fish, we can assure there's a very good chance you'll succeed *if you follow our directions closely*.

> *"Just think of what a novel, appreciated gift Bill would be for any of your bird-loving friends..."*

After all, *11* of the *19* testers had quick success with Bill. (Add me, that's 12 of 20.) And the remaining eight were highly optimistic they were close to success as we approached our deadline for this book.

It's worth noting that several of these eight as yet unsuccessful testers admitted that they hadn't followed our instructions as closely as they probably should have. Most of them were now going back for a second test, this time applying what they'd since learned from us and from the Field Editors who had succeeded.

So, we can't guarantee Bill will work for you. But I *can* guarantee that you, your whole family and likely even your neighbors will have a great deal of *fun* giving him a try. As I said in the beginning, Bill just may prove to be one of the best "conversation pieces" you ever put in your yard.

We Want to Hear from *YOU*

Yes, after you put Bill to "work" in your yard, we'd like you to share details of your trials, your suggestions, your pictures and, hopefully, your success with us.

We'll use the best of these comments in upcoming issues of *Birds & Blooms* magazine, where we'll certainly follow the saga of Bill in the months ahead.

And, if we receive as many exciting letters and photos from Bill users as we did from our Field Editors (90% of what's

"WHO'S THAT OUT THERE?" Testers said they'd glance out the window and be surprised to see "a man" there. Then they'd smile when they realized it was their friend Bill.

in this book came from only 21 people), we just may gather the best of them into another book. This second edition would likely be bigger than this one and feature full-color photos throughout.

So, this is your opportunity to be "published". Send your comments, suggestions and pictures to: "Bill Bird-in-Hand", *Birds & Blooms*, 5400 S. 60th St., Greendale WI 53129.

Or, you can E-mail us at *editors@birdsandblooms.com*.

Bill Makes a GREAT Gift

Whether or not you've yet ordered Bill for yourself, think of what a novel, appreciated gift this would be for any of your bird-loving friends! They'd remember this gift and talk about it (and you) every day as they watch the activity around Bill in their backyard.

Just maybe they'd like a copy of this book, too (hint, hint). Now that you've just finished reading your copy, you're in a good position to know whether they'd enjoy this book, and whether or not you should give them Bill as well.

Ordering Bill or the book for yourself or a gift is as easy as picking up your phone. Just have your credit card ready and dial toll-free **1-800/558-1013**.

You can also send your order to: Country Store, Suite 4387, P.O. Box 990, Greendale WI 53129. (Add 5% sales tax for orders shipped to Wisconsin.) Or you can order on-line via our Web site: *www.countrystorecatalog.com.*

Oh, did you say you wanted a subscription to *Birds & Blooms*, too, for yourself or as a gift for a friend? That's available by phone (1-800/344-6913) or by mail by sending your order to: *Birds & Blooms*, Reiman Publications, P.O. Box 5294, Harlan IA 51593. (We have some nice, hardworking rural folks there in Harlan who handle our mailed subscriptions for us.)

So…if you'd like to order any of these three items, here are the code numbers and the cost. (Note that it's $7.95 for shipping and guaranteed delivery of Bill; and $3.95 for shipping/delivery of the book. But if you order *both at once,* $7.95 covers shipping/delivery of both items.)

30355 "Bill Bird-in-Hand"…standing 5'8", made of durable weather-resistant material, with complete instructions for easy assembly and use
.......**$58.99** (plus $7.95 shipping and guaranteed delivery)

30795 Bill's for the Birds book…soft cover, 5-5/8" x 8-5/8"
.......**$11.99** (plus $3.95 shipping/guaranteed delivery)

Birds & Blooms magazine…1 year, six bimonthly issues
.......**$17.98** (Canadian subscription: $23.98)

30120 *Birds & Blooms* Squirrel-Proof Feeder, shown below
.......**$39.99** (plus $6.95 shipping and guaranteed delivery)

(To order, see details at left.)

SEND YOUR SQUIRRELS A MESSAGE with our one-of-a-kind *Birds & Blooms* Squirrel-Proof Feeder. The spring-loaded guard keeps the squirrels out of the feed and gives them a piece of your mind at the same time. The door above the feed tray stays open for birds, but when heavier squirrels climb aboard, the weight-activated door closes tight and at the same time reveals one of three fun messages (all included): *"Nuts to you, Mr. Squirrel!", "Birds—1, Squirrels—0",* and *"Sorry, Squirrel, No Free Lunch!"* It's sure to make your friends laugh, but squirrels won't find it that funny. Steel feeder holds 1-1/2 gallons of seed. Comes with a hanger and pole-mounting hardware.